THIS JOURNAL BELONGS TO

_____

60 Days of Gratefulness

A Gratitude Stimulating Workbook-Journal

ZBook Publishing, LLC
P.O. Box 2085
Stone Mountain, GA 30087
www.zbookpublishing.com

60 Days of Gratefulness
First Edition
ZBook Publishing, LLC

ISBN-13: 978-1-941689-05-9

"It's not happiness that brings us gratitude. It's gratitude that brings us happiness."

~ Anonymous

DAY 3

MORNING RITUAL

Today, I Am Feeling _____.

Today, I Will Accomplish _____.

I Love My _____.

☐ SAY THE FOLLOWING PROMPTS OUT LOUD AND
CHECK THE BOX ONCE COMPLETE:

> I INVITE GRATITUDE INTO MY HEART NOW
>
> I AM GRATEFUL FOR THIS BEAUTIFUL DAY
>
> I AM THANKFUL FOR EVERYTHING I HAVE
>
> I AM GRATEFUL FOR THE BLESSINGS THIS DAY
> WILL BRING
>
> I AM GRATEFUL FOR WHO I AM
>
> I AM GRATEFUL TO BE ALIVE
>
> I AM GRATEFUL TO HAVE ALL THE ANSWERS
> TO MY PROBLEMS

☐ Meditate for five minutes—in a quiet place—on all the things you
are grateful for

☐ Do five minutes of stretching

☐ Listen to positive songs

☐ Compliment someone today.

DAY 3

EVENING RITUAL

☐ LIST THREE GOOD THINGS THAT HAPPENED TODAY AND THEN ADD THEM TO THE GRATITUDE JAR.

Circle Three Feelings That Describe Your Mood Today		
Jovial	Hopeful	Bored
Happy	Excited	Creative
Nervous	Neutral	Ambitious
Tired	Depressed	Shy
Stressed	Anxious	Embarrassed
Scattered	Angry	Calm

Describe what brought about these feelings

_____

_____

_____

Who did you compliment today and how did that make you feel?

_____

_____

_____

REFLECTIONS

Detail everything you've loved about your day.

_____

_____

_____

_____

_____

_____

_____

_____

_____

Detail how you can make tomorrow an even better day.

_____

_____

_____

_____

_____

_____

_____

_____

_____

DAY 4

MORNING RITUAL

Today, I Am Feeling _____.

Today, I Will Accomplish _____.

I Love My _____.

☐ SAY THE FOLLOWING PROMPTS OUT LOUD AND
CHECK THE BOX ONCE COMPLETE:

> I INVITE GRATITUDE INTO MY HEART NOW
>
> I AM GRATEFUL FOR THIS BEAUTIFUL DAY
>
> I AM THANKFUL FOR EVERYTHING I HAVE
>
> I AM GRATEFUL FOR THE BLESSINGS THIS DAY
> WILL BRING
>
> I AM GRATEFUL FOR WHO I AM
>
> I AM GRATEFUL TO BE ALIVE
>
> I AM GRATEFUL TO HAVE ALL THE ANSWERS
> TO MY PROBLEMS

☐ Meditate for five minutes—in a quiet place—on all the things you
are grateful for

☐ Do five minutes of stretching

☐ Listen to positive songs

☐ Compliment someone today

DAY 4

EVENING RITUAL

☐ LIST THREE GOOD THINGS THAT HAPPENED TODAY, AND THEN ADD THEM TO THE GRATITUDE JAR.

Circle Three Feelings That Describe Your Mood Today

Jovial	Hopeful	Bored
Happy	Excited	Creative
Nervous	Neutral	Ambitious
Tired	Depressed	Shy
Stressed	Anxious	Embarrassed
Scattered	Angry	Calm

Describe what brought about these feelings

_____

_____

_____

Who did you compliment today and how did that make you feel?

_____

_____

_____

REFLECTIONS

What or who has made you smile this week and why?

_____

_____

_____

_____

_____

_____

_____

_____

_____

_____

_____

_____

_____

_____

_____

_____

_____

_____

_____

_____

_____

_____

_____

DAY 5

MORNING RITUAL

Today, I Am Feeling _____.

Today, I Will Accomplish _____.

I Love My _____.

☐ SAY THE FOLLOWING PROMPTS OUT LOUD AND CHECK THE BOX ONCE COMPLETE:

> I INVITE GRATITUDE INTO MY HEART NOW
>
> I AM GRATEFUL FOR THIS BEAUTIFUL DAY
>
> I AM THANKFUL FOR EVERYTHING I HAVE
>
> I AM GRATEFUL FOR THE BLESSINGS THIS DAY WILL BRING
>
> I AM GRATEFUL FOR WHO I AM
>
> I AM GRATEFUL TO BE ALIVE
>
> I AM GRATEFUL TO HAVE ALL THE ANSWERS TO MY PROBLEMS

☐ Meditate for five minutes—in a quiet place—on all the things you are grateful for

☐ Do five minutes of stretching

☐ Listen to positive songs

☐ Compliment someone today

DAY 5

EVENING RITUAL

☐ LIST THREE GOOD THINGS THAT HAPPENED TODAY, AND THEN ADD THEM TO THE GRATITUDE JAR.

Circle Three Feelings That Describe Your Mood Today		
Jovial	Hopeful	Bored
Happy	Excited	Creative
Nervous	Neutral	Ambitious
Tired	Depressed	Shy
Stressed	Anxious	Embarrassed
Scattered	Angry	Calm

Describe what brought about these feelings

_____

_____

_____

Who did you compliment today and how did that make you feel?

_____

_____

_____

REFLECTIONS

List the qualities and skills that you're grateful for.

_____

_____

_____

_____

_____

_____

_____

_____

_____

_____

_____

_____

_____

_____

_____

_____

_____

_____

_____

_____

_____

_____

_____

_____

DAY 6   DATE: __ / __ / __

MORNING RITUAL

Today, I Am Feeling _____.
Today, I Will Accomplish _____.
I Love My _____.

☐ SAY THE FOLLOWING PROMPTS OUT LOUD AND
   CHECK THE BOX ONCE COMPLETE:

   I INVITE GRATITUDE INTO MY HEART NOW
   I AM GRATEFUL FOR THIS BEAUTIFUL DAY
   I AM THANKFUL FOR EVERYTHING I HAVE
   I AM GRATEFUL FOR THE BLESSINGS THIS DAY
   WILL BRING
   I AM GRATEFUL FOR WHO I AM
   I AM GRATEFUL TO BE ALIVE
   I AM GRATEFUL TO HAVE ALL THE ANSWERS
   TO MY PROBLEMS

☐ Meditate for five minutes—in a quiet place—on all the things you
   are grateful for
☐ Do five minutes of stretching
☐ Listen to positive songs
☐ Compliment someone today

DAY 6

DATE: __ / __ / __

EVENING RITUAL

"He is a wise man who does not grieve for the things which he has not but rejoices for those which he has."

—Epictetus

☐ LIST THREE GOOD THINGS THAT HAPPENED TODAY AND THEN ADD THEM TO THE GRATITUDE JAR.

Circle Three Feelings That Describe Your Mood Today		
Jovial	Hopeful	Bored
Happy	Excited	Creative
Nervous	Neutral	Ambitious
Tired	Depressed	Shy
Stressed	Anxious	Embarrassed
Scattered	Angry	Calm

Describe what brought about these feelings

_____

_____

_____

Who did you compliment today and how did that make you feel?

_____

_____

_____

REFLECTIONS

Write out your personal definition of these words: happiness, love, and success, and why you're grateful for these experiences.

_____

_____

_____

_____

_____

_____

_____

_____

_____

_____

_____

_____

_____

_____

_____

_____

_____

_____

_____

_____

_____

_____

_____

_____

_____

"Strive to find things to be thankful for, and just look for the good in who you are."

-Bethany Hamilton

DAY 7

MORNING RITUAL

Today, I Am Feeling _____.

Today, I Will Accomplish _____.

I Love My _____.

☐ SAY THE FOLLOWING PROMPTS OUT LOUD AND CHECK THE BOX ONCE COMPLETE:

> I INVITE GRATITUDE INTO MY HEART NOW
>
> I AM GRATEFUL FOR THIS BEAUTIFUL DAY
>
> I AM THANKFUL FOR EVERYTHING I HAVE
>
> I AM GRATEFUL FOR THE BLESSINGS THIS DAY WILL BRING
>
> I AM GRATEFUL FOR WHO I AM
>
> I AM GRATEFUL TO BE ALIVE
>
> I AM GRATEFUL TO HAVE ALL THE ANSWERS TO MY PROBLEMS

☐ Meditate for five minutes—in a quiet place—on all the things you are grateful for

☐ Do five minutes of stretching

☐ Listen to positive songs

☐ Compliment someone today

DAY 7

DATE: __/__/__

EVENING RITUAL

☐ LIST THREE GOOD THINGS THAT HAPPENED TODAY
AND THEN ADD THEM TO THE GRATITUDE JAR.

Circle Three Feelings That Describe Your Mood Today		
Jovial	Hopeful	Bored
Happy	Excited	Creative
Nervous	Neutral	Ambitious
Tired	Depressed	Shy
Stressed	Anxious	Embarrassed
Scattered	Angry	Calm

Describe what brought about these feelings

_____

_____

_____

Who did you compliment today and how did that make you feel?

_____

_____

_____

REFLECTIONS

Document three of the best days of your life and why.

"*Appreciation is a wonderful thing.
It makes what is excellent in others
belong to us as well.*"

-Voltaire

DAY 8

MORNING RITUAL

Today, I Am Feeling _____.
Today, I Will Accomplish _____.
I Love My _____.

☐ SAY THE FOLLOWING PROMPTS OUT LOUD AND
   CHECK THE BOX ONCE COMPLETE:

> I INVITE GRATITUDE INTO MY HEART NOW
>
> I AM GRATEFUL FOR THIS BEAUTIFUL DAY
>
> I AM THANKFUL FOR EVERYTHING I HAVE
>
> I AM GRATEFUL FOR THE BLESSINGS THIS DAY
> WILL BRING
>
> I AM GRATEFUL FOR WHO I AM
>
> I AM GRATEFUL TO BE ALIVE
>
> I AM GRATEFUL TO HAVE ALL THE ANSWERS
> TO MY PROBLEMS

☐ Meditate for five minutes—in a quiet place—on all the things you
   are grateful for
☐ Do five minutes of stretching
☐ Listen to positive songs
☐ Compliment someone today

DAY 8

EVENING RITUAL

☐ LIST THREE GOOD THINGS THAT HAPPENED TODAY AND THEN ADD THEM TO THE GRATITUDE JAR.

Circle Three Feelings That Describe Your Mood Today		
Jovial	Hopeful	Bored
Happy	Excited	Creative
Nervous	Neutral	Ambitious
Tired	Depressed	Shy
Stressed	Anxious	Embarrassed
Scattered	Angry	Calm

Describe what brought about these feelings

_____

_____

_____

Who did you compliment today and how did that make you feel?

_____

_____

_____

REFLECTIONS

What do you love most about your career?

_____

_____

_____

_____

_____

_____

_____

_____

_____

_____

_____

_____

_____

_____

_____

_____

_____

_____

_____

_____

_____

_____

DAY 9

DATE: __ / __ / __

MORNING RITUAL

Today, I Am Feeling _____.

Today, I Will Accomplish _____.

I Love My _____.

☐ SAY THE FOLLOWING PROMPTS OUT LOUD AND CHECK THE BOX ONCE COMPLETE:

> I INVITE GRATITUDE INTO MY HEART NOW
>
> I AM GRATEFUL FOR THIS BEAUTIFUL DAY
>
> I AM THANKFUL FOR EVERYTHING I HAVE
>
> I AM GRATEFUL FOR THE BLESSINGS THIS DAY WILL BRING
>
> I AM GRATEFUL FOR WHO I AM
>
> I AM GRATEFUL TO BE ALIVE
>
> I AM GRATEFUL TO HAVE ALL THE ANSWERS TO MY PROBLEMS

☐ Meditate for five minutes—in a quiet place—on all the things you are grateful for

☐ Do five minutes of stretching

☐ Listen to positive songs

☐ Compliment someone today

DAY 9

EVENING RITUAL

☐ LIST THREE GOOD THINGS THAT HAPPENED TODAY AND THEN ADD THEM TO THE GRATITUDE JAR.

Circle Three Feelings That Describe Your Mood Today

Jovial	Hopeful	Bored
Happy	Excited	Creative
Nervous	Neutral	Ambitious
Tired	Depressed	Shy
Stressed	Anxious	Embarrassed
Scattered	Angry	Calm

Describe what brought about these feelings

_____

_____

_____

Who did you compliment today and how did that make you feel?

_____

_____

_____

REFLECTIONS

How do you show gratitude to your friends?

_____

_____

_____

_____

_____

_____

_____

_____

_____

_____

_____

_____

_____

_____

_____

_____

_____

_____

_____

_____

_____

_____

DAY 10

MORNING RITUAL

Today, I Am Feeling _____.
Today, I Will Accomplish _____.
I Love My _____.

☐ SAY THE FOLLOWING PROMPTS OUT LOUD AND CHECK THE BOX ONCE COMPLETE:

> I INVITE GRATITUDE INTO MY HEART NOW
>
> I AM GRATEFUL FOR THIS BEAUTIFUL DAY
>
> I AM THANKFUL FOR EVERYTHING I HAVE
>
> I AM GRATEFUL FOR THE BLESSINGS THIS DAY WILL BRING
>
> I AM GRATEFUL FOR WHO I AM
>
> I AM GRATEFUL TO BE ALIVE
>
> I AM GRATEFUL TO HAVE ALL THE ANSWERS TO MY PROBLEMS

☐ Meditate for five minutes—in a quiet place—on all the things you are grateful for
☐ Do five minutes of stretching
☐ Listen to positive songs
☐ Compliment someone today

DAY 10

EVENING RITUAL

☐ LIST THREE GOOD THINGS THAT HAPPENED TODAY AND THEN ADD THEM TO THE GRATITUDE JAR.

Circle Three Feelings That Describe Your Mood Today		
Jovial	Hopeful	Bored
Happy	Excited	Creative
Nervous	Neutral	Ambitious
Tired	Depressed	Shy
Stressed	Anxious	Embarrassed
Scattered	Angry	Calm

Describe what brought about these feelings

_____

_____

_____

Who did you compliment today and how did that make you feel?

_____

_____

_____

REFLECTIONS

What simple pleasures are you most thankful for in life?

_____

_____

_____

_____

_____

_____

_____

_____

_____

_____

What makes you the happiest?

_____

_____

_____

_____

_____

_____

_____

_____

_____

_____

DAY 11

MORNING RITUAL

Today, I Am Feeling _____.

Today, I Will Accomplish _____.

I Love My _____.

☐ SAY THE FOLLOWING PROMPTS OUT LOUD AND CHECK THE BOX ONCE COMPLETE:

> I INVITE GRATITUDE INTO MY HEART NOW
>
> I AM GRATEFUL FOR THIS BEAUTIFUL DAY
>
> I AM THANKFUL FOR EVERYTHING I HAVE
>
> I AM GRATEFUL FOR THE BLESSINGS THIS DAY WILL BRING
>
> I AM GRATEFUL FOR WHO I AM
>
> I AM GRATEFUL TO BE ALIVE
>
> I AM GRATEFUL TO HAVE ALL THE ANSWERS TO MY PROBLEMS

☐ Meditate for five minutes—in a quiet place—on all the things you are grateful for

☐ Do five minutes of stretching

☐ Listen to positive songs

☐ Compliment someone today

DAY 11   DATE: __ / __ / __

EVENING RITUAL

FILL THE GRATITUDE JAR EVERY NIGHT

☐ LIST THREE GOOD THINGS THAT HAPPENED TODAY
AND THEN ADD THEM TO THE GRATITUDE JAR.

Circle Three Feelings That Describe Your Mood Today		
Jovial	Hopeful	Bored
Happy	Excited	Creative
Nervous	Neutral	Ambitious
Tired	Depressed	Shy
Stressed	Anxious	Embarrassed
Scattered	Angry	Calm

Describe what brought about these feelings

_____

_____

_____

Who did you compliment today and how did that make you feel?

_____

_____

_____

REFLECTIONS

List all of the people that have helped you in some way in life.

_____

_____

_____

_____

_____

_____

_____

_____

_____

_____

_____

_____

_____

_____

_____

_____

_____

_____

_____

_____

_____

_____

_____

_____

_____

_____

DAY 12

MORNING RITUAL

Today, I Am Feeling _____.

Today, I Will Accomplish _____.

I Love My _____.

☐ SAY THE FOLLOWING PROMPTS OUT LOUD AND CHECK THE BOX ONCE COMPLETE:

I INVITE GRATITUDE INTO MY HEART NOW

I AM GRATEFUL FOR THIS BEAUTIFUL DAY

I AM THANKFUL FOR EVERYTHING I HAVE

I AM GRATEFUL FOR THE BLESSINGS THIS DAY WILL BRING

I AM GRATEFUL FOR WHO I AM

I AM GRATEFUL TO BE ALIVE

I AM GRATEFUL TO HAVE ALL THE ANSWERS TO MY PROBLEMS

☐ Meditate for five minutes—in a quiet place—on all the things you are grateful for

☐ Do five minutes of stretching

☐ Listen to positive songs

☐ Compliment someone today

DAY 12

EVENING RITUAL

☐ LIST THREE GOOD THINGS THAT HAPPENED TODAY AND THEN ADD THEM TO THE GRATITUDE JAR.

Circle Three Feelings That Describe Your Mood Today		
Jovial	Hopeful	Bored
Happy	Excited	Creative
Nervous	Neutral	Ambitious
Tired	Depressed	Shy
Stressed	Anxious	Embarrassed
Scattered	Angry	Calm

Describe what brought about these feelings

_____

_____

_____

Who did you compliment today and how did that make you feel?

_____

_____

_____

REFLECTIONS

List the things you can do this week to make a difference in somebody else's life.

_____

_____

_____

_____

_____

_____

_____

_____

_____

List the ways that you can serve others, and who they would be.

_____

_____

_____

_____

_____

_____

_____

_____

_____

DAY 13

MORNING RITUAL

Today, I Am Feeling _____.

Today, I Will Accomplish _____.

I Love My _____.

☐ SAY THE FOLLOWING PROMPTS OUT LOUD AND CHECK THE BOX ONCE COMPLETE:

> I INVITE GRATITUDE INTO MY HEART NOW
>
> I AM GRATEFUL FOR THIS BEAUTIFUL DAY
>
> I AM THANKFUL FOR EVERYTHING I HAVE
>
> I AM GRATEFUL FOR THE BLESSINGS THIS DAY WILL BRING
>
> I AM GRATEFUL FOR WHO I AM
>
> I AM GRATEFUL TO BE ALIVE
>
> I AM GRATEFUL TO HAVE ALL THE ANSWERS TO MY PROBLEMS

☐ Meditate for five minutes—in a quiet place—on all the things you are grateful for

☐ Do five minutes of stretching

☐ Listen to positive songs

☐ Compliment someone today

DAY 13

EVENING RITUAL

☐ LIST THREE GOOD THINGS THAT HAPPENED TODAY
AND THEN ADD THEM TO THE GRATITUDE JAR.

Circle Three Feelings That Describe Your Mood Today		
Jovial	Hopeful	Bored
Happy	Excited	Creative
Nervous	Neutral	Ambitious
Tired	Depressed	Shy
Stressed	Anxious	Embarrassed
Scattered	Angry	Calm

Describe what brought about these feelings

_____

_____

_____

Who did you compliment today and how did that make you feel?

_____

_____

_____

REFLECTIONS

What failure or mistake are you grateful for in life and why?

_____

_____

_____

_____

_____

_____

_____

_____

_____

_____

_____

_____

_____

_____

_____

_____

_____

_____

_____

_____

_____

_____

_____

_____

"When you are grateful, fear disappears, and abundance appears."

-Anthony Robbins

DAY 14

MORNING RITUAL

Today, I Am Feeling _____.

Today, I Will Accomplish _____.

I Love My _____.

☐ SAY THE FOLLOWING PROMPTS OUT LOUD AND CHECK THE BOX ONCE COMPLETE:

> I INVITE GRATITUDE INTO MY HEART NOW
>
> I AM GRATEFUL FOR THIS BEAUTIFUL DAY
>
> I AM THANKFUL FOR EVERYTHING I HAVE
>
> I AM GRATEFUL FOR THE BLESSINGS THIS DAY WILL BRING
>
> I AM GRATEFUL FOR WHO I AM
>
> I AM GRATEFUL TO BE ALIVE
>
> I AM GRATEFUL TO HAVE ALL THE ANSWERS TO MY PROBLEMS

☐ Meditate for five minutes—in a quiet place—on all the things you are grateful for

☐ Do five minutes of stretching

☐ Listen to positive songs

☐ Compliment someone today

DAY 14

EVENING RITUAL

☐ LIST THREE GOOD THINGS THAT HAPPENED TODAY AND THEN ADD THEM TO THE GRATITUDE JAR.

Circle Three Feelings That Describe Your Mood Today		
Jovial	Hopeful	Bored
Happy	Excited	Creative
Nervous	Neutral	Ambitious
Tired	Depressed	Shy
Stressed	Anxious	Embarrassed
Scattered	Angry	Calm

Describe what brought about these feelings

_____

_____

_____

Who did you compliment today and how did that make you feel?

_____

_____

_____

REFLECTIONS

What have you accomplished today?

_____

_____

_____

_____

_____

_____

_____

_____

_____

_____

_____

_____

_____

_____

_____

_____

_____

_____

_____

_____

_____

_____

"Gratitude opens the door to the power, the wisdom, the creativity of the universe. You open the door through gratitude."

~ Deepak Chopra

DAY 15

DATE: __ /__ /__

MORNING RITUAL

Today, I Am Feeling _____.
Today, I Will Accomplish _____.
I Love My _____.

☐ SAY THE FOLLOWING PROMPTS OUT LOUD AND CHECK THE BOX ONCE COMPLETE:

> I INVITE GRATITUDE INTO MY HEART NOW
>
> I AM GRATEFUL FOR THIS BEAUTIFUL DAY
>
> I AM THANKFUL FOR EVERYTHING I HAVE
>
> I AM GRATEFUL FOR THE BLESSINGS THIS DAY WILL BRING
>
> I AM GRATEFUL FOR WHO I AM
>
> I AM GRATEFUL TO BE ALIVE
>
> I AM GRATEFUL TO HAVE ALL THE ANSWERS TO MY PROBLEMS

☐ Meditate for five minutes—in a quiet place—on all the things you are grateful for
☐ Do five minutes of stretching
☐ Listen to positive songs
☐ Compliment someone today

DAY 15

EVENING RITUAL

☐ LIST THREE GOOD THINGS THAT HAPPENED TODAY
AND THEN ADD THEM TO THE GRATITUDE JAR.

Circle Three Feelings That Describe Your Mood Today

Jovial	Hopeful	Bored
Happy	Excited	Creative
Nervous	Neutral	Ambitious
Tired	Depressed	Shy
Stressed	Anxious	Embarrassed
Scattered	Angry	Calm

Describe what brought about these feelings

_____

_____

_____

Who did you compliment today and how did that make you feel?

_____

_____

_____

REFLECTIONS

Write out your current goals. What skills and qualities are you grateful for that can help you to reach them?

_____

_____

_____

_____

_____

_____

_____

_____

_____

_____

_____

_____

_____

_____

_____

_____

_____

_____

_____

_____

_____

_____

DAY 16

MORNING RITUAL

Today, I Am Feeling _____.

Today, I Will Accomplish _____.

I Love My _____.

☐ SAY THE FOLLOWING PROMPTS OUT LOUD AND CHECK THE BOX ONCE COMPLETE:

> I INVITE GRATITUDE INTO MY HEART NOW
>
> I AM GRATEFUL FOR THIS BEAUTIFUL DAY
>
> I AM THANKFUL FOR EVERYTHING I HAVE
>
> I AM GRATEFUL FOR THE BLESSINGS THIS DAY
> WILL BRING
>
> I AM GRATEFUL FOR WHO I AM
>
> I AM GRATEFUL TO BE ALIVE
>
> I AM GRATEFUL TO HAVE ALL THE ANSWERS
> TO MY PROBLEMS

☐ Meditate for five minutes—in a quiet place—on all the things you are grateful for

☐ Do five minutes of stretching

☐ Listen to positive songs

☐ Compliment someone today

DAY 16

EVENING RITUAL

☐ LIST THREE GOOD THINGS THAT HAPPENED TODAY AND THEN ADD THEM TO THE GRATITUDE JAR.

Circle Three Feelings That Describe Your Mood Today		
Jovial	Hopeful	Bored
Happy	Excited	Creative
Nervous	Neutral	Ambitious
Tired	Depressed	Shy
Stressed	Anxious	Embarrassed
Scattered	Angry	Calm

Describe what brought about these feelings

_____

_____

_____

Who did you compliment today and how did that make you feel?

_____

_____

_____

REFLECTIONS

Write a list of the people you admire in life and why.

DAY 17

MORNING RITUAL

Today, I Am Feeling _____.

Today, I Will Accomplish _____.

I Love My _____.

☐ SAY THE FOLLOWING PROMPTS OUT LOUD AND CHECK THE BOX ONCE COMPLETE:

> I INVITE GRATITUDE INTO MY HEART NOW
>
> I AM GRATEFUL FOR THIS BEAUTIFUL DAY
>
> I AM THANKFUL FOR EVERYTHING I HAVE
>
> I AM GRATEFUL FOR THE BLESSINGS THIS DAY WILL BRING
>
> I AM GRATEFUL FOR WHO I AM
>
> I AM GRATEFUL TO BE ALIVE
>
> I AM GRATEFUL TO HAVE ALL THE ANSWERS TO MY PROBLEMS

☐ Meditate for five minutes—in a quiet place—on all the things you are grateful for

☐ Do five minutes of stretching

☐ Listen to positive songs

☐ Compliment someone today

DAY 17

DATE: __ / __ / __

EVENING RITUAL

☐ LIST THREE GOOD THINGS THAT HAPPENED TODAY
AND THEN ADD THEM TO THE GRATITUDE JAR.

Circle Three Feelings That Describe Your Mood Today

Jovial	Hopeful	Bored
Happy	Excited	Creative
Nervous	Neutral	Ambitious
Tired	Depressed	Shy
Stressed	Anxious	Embarrassed
Scattered	Angry	Calm

Describe what brought about these feelings

_____

_____

_____

Who did you compliment today and how did that make you feel?

_____

_____

_____

REFLECTIONS

What does your ideal day look like? Be as specific and detailed as you can here and list the reasons why.

_____

_____

_____

_____

_____

_____

_____

_____

_____

_____

_____

_____

_____

_____

_____

_____

_____

_____

_____

_____

_____

_____

_____

_____

DAY 18

MORNING RITUAL

Today, I Am Feeling _____.

Today, I Will Accomplish _____.

I Love My _____.

☐ SAY THE FOLLOWING PROMPTS OUT LOUD AND
CHECK THE BOX ONCE COMPLETE:

> I INVITE GRATITUDE INTO MY HEART NOW
>
> I AM GRATEFUL FOR THIS BEAUTIFUL DAY
>
> I AM THANKFUL FOR EVERYTHING I HAVE
>
> I AM GRATEFUL FOR THE BLESSINGS THIS DAY
> WILL BRING
>
> I AM GRATEFUL FOR WHO I AM
>
> I AM GRATEFUL TO BE ALIVE
>
> I AM GRATEFUL TO HAVE ALL THE ANSWERS
> TO MY PROBLEMS

☐ Meditate for five minutes—in a quiet place—on all the things you
are grateful for

☐ Do five minutes of stretching

☐ Listen to positive songs

☐ Compliment someone today

DAY 18

EVENING RITUAL

☐ LIST THREE GOOD THINGS THAT HAPPENED TODAY
AND THEN ADD THEM TO THE GRATITUDE JAR.

Circle Three Feelings That Describe Your Mood Today		
Jovial	Hopeful	Bored
Happy	Excited	Creative
Nervous	Neutral	Ambitious
Tired	Depressed	Shy
Stressed	Anxious	Embarrassed
Scattered	Angry	Calm

Describe what brought about these feelings

_____

_____

_____

Who did you compliment today and how did that make you feel?

_____

_____

_____

REFLECTIONS

Write out your deepest desires for yourself or your life.

_____

_____

_____

_____

_____

_____

_____

_____

_____

_____

_____

_____

_____

_____

_____

_____

_____

_____

_____

_____

_____

_____

_____

_____

_____

DAY 19

MORNING RITUAL

"It's not happiness that brings us gratitude. It's gratitude that brings us happiness."

— Anonymous

Today, I Am Feeling _____.

Today, I Will Accomplish _____.

I Love My _____.

☐ SAY THE FOLLOWING PROMPTS OUT LOUD AND CHECK THE BOX ONCE COMPLETE:

> I INVITE GRATITUDE INTO MY HEART NOW
>
> I AM GRATEFUL FOR THIS BEAUTIFUL DAY
>
> I AM THANKFUL FOR EVERYTHING I HAVE
>
> I AM GRATEFUL FOR THE BLESSINGS THIS DAY WILL BRING
>
> I AM GRATEFUL FOR WHO I AM
>
> I AM GRATEFUL TO BE ALIVE
>
> I AM GRATEFUL TO HAVE ALL THE ANSWERS TO MY PROBLEMS

☐ Meditate for five minutes—in a quiet place—on all the things you are grateful for

☐ Do five minutes of stretching

☐ Listen to positive songs

☐ Compliment someone today

DAY 19

EVENING RITUAL

☐ LIST THREE GOOD THINGS THAT HAPPENED TODAY
AND THEN ADD THEM TO THE GRATITUDE JAR.

Circle Three Feelings That Describe Your Mood Today		
Jovial	Hopeful	Bored
Happy	Excited	Creative
Nervous	Neutral	Ambitious
Tired	Depressed	Shy
Stressed	Anxious	Embarrassed
Scattered	Angry	Calm

Describe what brought about these feelings

_____

_____

_____

Who did you compliment today and how did that make you feel?

_____

_____

_____

REFLECTIONS

Describe all of your favorite senses; the smells, tastes, sights, sounds, and feelings that you're grateful for.

DAY 20

MORNING RITUAL

Today, I Am Feeling _____.

Today, I Will Accomplish _____.

I Love My _____.

☐ SAY THE FOLLOWING PROMPTS OUT LOUD AND CHECK THE BOX ONCE COMPLETE:

    I INVITE GRATITUDE INTO MY HEART NOW

    I AM GRATEFUL FOR THIS BEAUTIFUL DAY

    I AM THANKFUL FOR EVERYTHING I HAVE

    I AM GRATEFUL FOR THE BLESSINGS THIS DAY WILL BRING

    I AM GRATEFUL FOR WHO I AM

    I AM GRATEFUL TO BE ALIVE

    I AM GRATEFUL TO HAVE ALL THE ANSWERS TO MY PROBLEMS

☐ Meditate for five minutes—in a quiet place—on all the things you are grateful for

☐ Do five minutes of stretching

☐ Listen to positive songs

☐ Compliment someone today

DAY 20

DATE: _ / _ / _

EVENING RITUAL

☐ LIST THREE GOOD THINGS THAT HAPPENED TODAY
AND THEN ADD THEM TO THE GRATITUDE JAR.

Circle Three Feelings That Describe Your Mood Today		
Jovial	Hopeful	Bored
Happy	Excited	Creative
Nervous	Neutral	Ambitious
Tired	Depressed	Shy
Stressed	Anxious	Embarrassed
Scattered	Angry	Calm

Describe what brought about these feelings

_____

_____

_____

Who did you compliment today and how did that make you feel?

_____

_____

_____

REFLECTIONS

What are twenty things you're looking forward to or would like to accomplish this year?

_____

_____

_____

_____

_____

_____

_____

_____

_____

_____

_____

_____

_____

_____

_____

_____

_____

_____

_____

_____

_____

_____

_____

"*Gratitude can transform
common days into thanksgivings,
turn routine jobs into joy,
and change ordinary opportunities
into blessings.*"

—William Arthur Ward

DAY 21

MORNING RITUAL

Today, I Am Feeling _____.

Today, I Will Accomplish _____.

I Love My _____.

☐ SAY THE FOLLOWING PROMPTS OUT LOUD AND CHECK THE BOX ONCE COMPLETE:

> I INVITE GRATITUDE INTO MY HEART NOW
>
> I AM GRATEFUL FOR THIS BEAUTIFUL DAY
>
> I AM THANKFUL FOR EVERYTHING I HAVE
>
> I AM GRATEFUL FOR THE BLESSINGS THIS DAY WILL BRING
>
> I AM GRATEFUL FOR WHO I AM
>
> I AM GRATEFUL TO BE ALIVE
>
> I AM GRATEFUL TO HAVE ALL THE ANSWERS TO MY PROBLEMS

☐ Meditate for five minutes—in a quiet place—on all the things you are grateful for

☐ Do five minutes of stretching

☐ Listen to a positive song

☐ Compliment someone today

DAY 21

EVENING RITUAL

☐ LIST THREE GOOD THINGS THAT HAPPENED TODAY
AND THEN ADD THEM TO THE GRATITUDE JAR.

Circle Three Feelings That Describe Your Mood Today		
Jovial	Hopeful	Bored
Happy	Excited	Creative
Nervous	Neutral	Ambitious
Tired	Depressed	Shy
Stressed	Anxious	Embarrassed
Scattered	Angry	Calm

Describe what brought about these feelings

_____

_____

_____

Who did you compliment today and how did that make you feel?

_____

_____

_____

REFLECTIONS

Describe a time you were proud of yourself for making a good choice.

DAY 22

MORNING RITUAL

Today, I Am Feeling _____.

Today, I Will Accomplish _____.

I Love My _____.

☐ SAY THE FOLLOWING PROMPTS OUT LOUD AND CHECK THE BOX ONCE COMPLETE:

> I INVITE GRATITUDE INTO MY HEART NOW
>
> I AM GRATEFUL FOR THIS BEAUTIFUL DAY
>
> I AM THANKFUL FOR EVERYTHING I HAVE
>
> I AM GRATEFUL FOR THE BLESSINGS THIS DAY WILL BRING
>
> I AM GRATEFUL FOR WHO I AM
>
> I AM GRATEFUL TO BE ALIVE
>
> I AM GRATEFUL TO HAVE ALL THE ANSWERS TO MY PROBLEMS

☐ Meditate for five minutes—in a quiet place—on all the things you are grateful for

☐ Do five minutes of stretching

☐ Listen to positive songs

☐ Compliment someone today

DAY 22

DATE: __ /__ /__

EVENING RITUAL

☐ LIST THREE GOOD THINGS THAT HAPPENED TODAY
AND THEN ADD THEM TO THE GRATITUDE JAR.

Circle Three Feelings That Describe Your Mood Today		
Jovial	Hopeful	Bored
Happy	Excited	Creative
Nervous	Neutral	Ambitious
Tired	Depressed	Shy
Stressed	Anxious	Embarrassed
Scattered	Angry	Calm

Describe what brought about these feelings

_____

_____

_____

Who did you compliment today and how did that make you feel?

_____

_____

_____

REFLECTIONS

What are you happy you don't have in your life and why?

_____

_____

_____

_____

_____

_____

_____

_____

_____

_____

_____

_____

_____

_____

_____

_____

_____

_____

_____

_____

_____

_____

_____

_____

DAY 23

MORNING RITUAL

Today, I Am Feeling _____.

Today, I Will Accomplish _____.

I Love My _____.

☐ SAY THE FOLLOWING PROMPTS OUT LOUD AND CHECK THE BOX ONCE COMPLETE:

> I INVITE GRATITUDE INTO MY HEART NOW
>
> I AM GRATEFUL FOR THIS BEAUTIFUL DAY
>
> I AM THANKFUL FOR EVERYTHING I HAVE
>
> I AM GRATEFUL FOR THE BLESSINGS THIS DAY WILL BRING
>
> I AM GRATEFUL FOR WHO I AM
>
> I AM GRATEFUL TO BE ALIVE
>
> I AM GRATEFUL TO HAVE ALL THE ANSWERS TO MY PROBLEMS

☐ Meditate for five minutes—in a quiet place—on all the things you are grateful for

☐ Do five minutes of stretching

☐ Listen to positive songs

☐ Compliment someone today

DAY 23

EVENING RITUAL

"He is a wise man who does not grieve for the things
which he has not but rejoices for those which he has."

—Epictetus

☐ LIST THREE GOOD THINGS THAT HAPPENED TODAY
AND THEN ADD THEM TO THE GRATITUDE JAR.

Circle Three Feelings That Describe Your Mood Today		
Jovial	Hopeful	Bored
Happy	Excited	Creative
Nervous	Neutral	Ambitious
Tired	Depressed	Shy
Stressed	Anxious	Embarrassed
Scattered	Angry	Calm

Describe what brought about these feelings

_____

_____

_____

Who did you compliment today and how did that make you feel?

_____

_____

_____

REFLECTIONS

Is there anything you can forgive yourself for and be grateful for the lesson?

_____

_____

_____

_____

_____

_____

_____

_____

_____

_____

_____

_____

_____

_____

_____

_____

_____

_____

_____

_____

_____

_____

_____

_____

_____

DAY 24

MORNING RITUAL

Today, I Am Feeling _____.

Today, I Will Accomplish _____.

I Love My _____.

☐ SAY THE FOLLOWING PROMPTS OUT LOUD AND CHECK THE BOX ONCE COMPLETE:

> I INVITE GRATITUDE INTO MY HEART NOW
>
> I AM GRATEFUL FOR THIS BEAUTIFUL DAY
>
> I AM THANKFUL FOR EVERYTHING I HAVE
>
> I AM GRATEFUL FOR THE BLESSINGS THIS DAY WILL BRING
>
> I AM GRATEFUL FOR WHO I AM
>
> I AM GRATEFUL TO BE ALIVE
>
> I AM GRATEFUL TO HAVE ALL THE ANSWERS TO MY PROBLEMS

☐ Meditate for five minutes—in a quiet place—on all the things you are grateful for

☐ Do five minutes of stretching

☐ Listen to positive songs

☐ Compliment someone today

DAY 24

EVENING RITUAL

☐ LIST THREE GOOD THINGS THAT HAPPENED TODAY
AND THEN ADD THEM TO THE GRATITUDE JAR.

Circle Three Feelings That Describe Your Mood Today

Jovial	Hopeful	Bored
Happy	Excited	Creative
Nervous	Neutral	Ambitious
Tired	Depressed	Shy
Stressed	Anxious	Embarrassed
Scattered	Angry	Calm

Describe what brought about these feelings

_____

_____

_____

Who did you compliment today and how did that make you feel?

_____

_____

_____

REFLECTIONS

Name a time you lucked out.

_____

_____

_____

_____

_____

_____

_____

_____

_____

_____

_____

_____

_____

_____

_____

_____

_____

_____

_____

_____

_____

_____

DAY 25

MORNING RITUAL

Today, I Am Feeling _____.
Today, I Will Accomplish _____.
I Love My _____.

☐ SAY THE FOLLOWING PROMPTS OUT LOUD AND
CHECK THE BOX ONCE COMPLETE:

> I INVITE GRATITUDE INTO MY HEART NOW
>
> I AM GRATEFUL FOR THIS BEAUTIFUL DAY
>
> I AM THANKFUL FOR EVERYTHING I HAVE
>
> I AM GRATEFUL FOR THE BLESSINGS THIS DAY
> WILL BRING
>
> I AM GRATEFUL FOR WHO I AM
>
> I AM GRATEFUL TO BE ALIVE
>
> I AM GRATEFUL TO HAVE ALL THE ANSWERS
> TO MY PROBLEMS

☐ Meditate for five minutes—in a quiet place—on all the things you
are grateful for
☐ Do five minutes of stretching
☐ Listen to positive songs
☐ Compliment someone today

DAY 25

EVENING RITUAL

☐ LIST THREE GOOD THINGS THAT HAPPENED TODAY
AND THEN ADD THEM TO THE GRATITUDE JAR.

Circle Three Feelings That Describe Your Mood Today		
Jovial	Hopeful	Bored
Happy	Excited	Creative
Nervous	Neutral	Ambitious
Tired	Depressed	Shy
Stressed	Anxious	Embarrassed
Scattered	Angry	Calm

Describe what brought about these feelings

_____

_____

_____

Who did you compliment today and how did that make you feel?

_____

_____

_____

REFLECTIONS

Write about the best decisions you've ever made.

DAY 26

MORNING RITUAL

Today, I Am Feeling _____.

Today, I Will Accomplish _____.

I Love My _____.

☐ SAY THE FOLLOWING PROMPTS OUT LOUD AND
   CHECK THE BOX ONCE COMPLETE:

> I INVITE GRATITUDE INTO MY HEART NOW
>
> I AM GRATEFUL FOR THIS BEAUTIFUL DAY
>
> I AM THANKFUL FOR EVERYTHING I HAVE
>
> I AM GRATEFUL FOR THE BLESSINGS THIS DAY
> WILL BRING
>
> I AM GRATEFUL FOR WHO I AM
>
> I AM GRATEFUL TO BE ALIVE
>
> I AM GRATEFUL TO HAVE ALL THE ANSWERS
> TO MY PROBLEMS

☐ Meditate for five minutes—in a quiet place—on all the things you
   are grateful for
☐ Do five minutes of stretching
☐ Listen to positive songs
☐ Compliment someone today

DAY 26

DATE: __ /__ /__

EVENING RITUAL

☐ LIST THREE GOOD THINGS THAT HAPPENED TODAY
AND THEN ADD THEM TO THE GRATITUDE JAR.

Circle Three Feelings That Describe Your Mood Today

Jovial	Hopeful	Bored
Happy	Excited	Creative
Nervous	Neutral	Ambitious
Tired	Depressed	Shy
Stressed	Anxious	Embarrassed
Scattered	Angry	Calm

Describe what brought about these feelings

_____

_____

_____

Who did you compliment today and how did that make you feel?

_____

_____

_____

REFLECTIONS

Name 3 things you like about your personality.

_____

_____

_____

_____

_____

_____

_____

_____

_____

_____

_____

_____

_____

_____

_____

_____

_____

_____

_____

_____

_____

DAY 27

MORNING RITUAL

Today, I Am Feeling _____.

Today, I Will Accomplish _____.

I Love My _____.

☐ SAY THE FOLLOWING PROMPTS OUT LOUD AND CHECK THE BOX ONCE COMPLETE:

> I INVITE GRATITUDE INTO MY HEART NOW
>
> I AM GRATEFUL FOR THIS BEAUTIFUL DAY
>
> I AM THANKFUL FOR EVERYTHING I HAVE
>
> I AM GRATEFUL FOR THE BLESSINGS THIS DAY WILL BRING
>
> I AM GRATEFUL FOR WHO I AM
>
> I AM GRATEFUL TO BE ALIVE
>
> I AM GRATEFUL TO HAVE ALL THE ANSWERS TO MY PROBLEMS

☐ Meditate for five minutes—in a quiet place—on all the things you are grateful for

☐ Do five minutes of stretching

☐ Listen to positive songs

☐ Compliment someone today

DAY 27

DATE: __ /__ /__

EVENING RITUAL

☐ LIST THREE GOOD THINGS THAT HAPPENED TODAY
AND THEN ADD THEM TO THE GRATITUDE JAR.

Circle Three Feelings That Describe Your Mood Today		
Jovial	Hopeful	Bored
Happy	Excited	Creative
Nervous	Neutral	Ambitious
Tired	Depressed	Shy
Stressed	Anxious	Embarrassed
Scattered	Angry	Calm

Describe what brought about these feelings

_____

_____

_____

Who did you compliment today and how did that make you feel?

_____

_____

_____

REFLECTIONS

Write about the best day of your life.

_____

_____

_____

_____

_____

_____

_____

_____

_____

_____

_____

_____

_____

_____

_____

_____

_____

_____

_____

_____

_____

_____

_____

_____

"He is a wise man who does not grieve for the things which he has not but rejoices for those which he has."

-Epictetus

DAY 28

MORNING RITUAL

Today, I Am Feeling _____.

Today, I Will Accomplish _____.

I Love My _____.

☐ SAY THE FOLLOWING PROMPTS OUT LOUD AND CHECK THE BOX ONCE COMPLETE:

> I INVITE GRATITUDE INTO MY HEART NOW
>
> I AM GRATEFUL FOR THIS BEAUTIFUL DAY
>
> I AM THANKFUL FOR EVERYTHING I HAVE
>
> I AM GRATEFUL FOR THE BLESSINGS THIS DAY
> WILL BRING
>
> I AM GRATEFUL FOR WHO I AM
>
> I AM GRATEFUL TO BE ALIVE
>
> I AM GRATEFUL TO HAVE ALL THE ANSWERS
> TO MY PROBLEMS

☐ Meditate for five minutes—in a quiet place—on all the things you are grateful for

☐ Do five minutes of stretching

☐ Listen to positive songs

☐ Compliment someone today

DAY 28

DATE: __/__/__

EVENING RITUAL

☐ LIST THREE GOOD THINGS THAT HAPPENED TODAY
AND THEN ADD THEM TO THE GRATITUDE JAR.

Circle Three Feelings That Describe Your Mood Today		
Jovial	Hopeful	Bored
Happy	Excited	Creative
Nervous	Neutral	Ambitious
Tired	Depressed	Shy
Stressed	Anxious	Embarrassed
Scattered	Angry	Calm

Describe what brought about these feelings

_____

_____

_____

Who did you compliment today and how did that make you feel?

_____

_____

_____

REFLECTIONS

List something you love about three family members and explain why.

_____

_____

_____

_____

_____

_____

_____

_____

_____

_____

_____

_____

_____

_____

_____

_____

_____

_____

_____

_____

_____

_____

DAY 29 DATE: __ / __ / __

MORNING RITUAL

Today, I Am Feeling _____.

Today, I Will Accomplish _____.

I Love My _____.

☐ SAY THE FOLLOWING PROMPTS OUT LOUD AND CHECK THE BOX ONCE COMPLETE:

> I INVITE GRATITUDE INTO MY HEART NOW
>
> I AM GRATEFUL FOR THIS BEAUTIFUL DAY
>
> I AM THANKFUL FOR EVERYTHING I HAVE
>
> I AM GRATEFUL FOR THE BLESSINGS THIS DAY WILL BRING
>
> I AM GRATEFUL FOR WHO I AM
>
> I AM GRATEFUL TO BE ALIVE
>
> I AM GRATEFUL TO HAVE ALL THE ANSWERS TO MY PROBLEMS

☐ Meditate for five minutes—in a quiet place—on all the things you are grateful for

☐ Do five minutes of stretching

☐ Listen to positive songs

☐ Compliment someone today

DAY 29

EVENING RITUAL

☐ LIST THREE GOOD THINGS THAT HAPPENED TODAY AND THEN ADD THEM TO THE GRATITUDE JAR.

Circle Three Feelings That Describe Your Mood Today		
Jovial	Hopeful	Bored
Happy	Excited	Creative
Nervous	Neutral	Ambitious
Tired	Depressed	Shy
Stressed	Anxious	Embarrassed
Scattered	Angry	Calm

Describe what brought about these feelings

_____

_____

_____

Who did you compliment today and how did that make you feel?

_____

_____

_____

REFLECTIONS

Write about what you've loved the most about each decade you've lived in.

_____

_____

_____

_____

_____

_____

_____

_____

_____

_____

_____

_____

_____

_____

_____

_____

_____

_____

_____

_____

_____

_____

DAY 30

MORNING RITUAL

Today, I Am Feeling _____.

Today, I Will Accomplish _____.

I Love My _____.

☐ SAY THE FOLLOWING PROMPTS OUT LOUD AND CHECK THE BOX ONCE COMPLETE:

> I INVITE GRATITUDE INTO MY HEART NOW
>
> I AM GRATEFUL FOR THIS BEAUTIFUL DAY
>
> I AM THANKFUL FOR EVERYTHING I HAVE
>
> I AM GRATEFUL FOR THE BLESSINGS THIS DAY
> WILL BRING
>
> I AM GRATEFUL FOR WHO I AM
>
> I AM GRATEFUL TO BE ALIVE
>
> I AM GRATEFUL TO HAVE ALL THE ANSWERS
> TO MY PROBLEMS

☐ Meditate for five minutes—in a quiet place—on all the things you are grateful for

☐ Do five minutes of stretching

☐ Listen to positive songs

☐ Compliment someone today

DAY 30

DATE: __/__/__

EVENING RITUAL

☐ LIST THREE GOOD THINGS THAT HAPPENED TODAY
AND THEN ADD THEM TO THE GRATITUDE JAR.

Circle Three Feelings That Describe Your Mood Today		
Jovial	Hopeful	Bored
Happy	Excited	Creative
Nervous	Neutral	Ambitious
Tired	Depressed	Shy
Stressed	Anxious	Embarrassed
Scattered	Angry	Calm

Describe what brought about these feelings

_____

_____

_____

Who did you compliment today and how did that make you feel?

_____

_____

_____

REFLECTIONS

Write about any spiritual practices that make you feel good.

_____

_____

_____

_____

_____

_____

_____

_____

_____

_____

_____

_____

_____

_____

_____

_____

_____

_____

_____

_____

_____

_____

_____

_____

DAY 31

MORNING RITUAL

Today, I Am Feeling _____.

Today, I Will Accomplish _____.

I Love My _____.

☐ SAY THE FOLLOWING PROMPTS OUT LOUD AND CHECK THE BOX ONCE COMPLETE:

> I INVITE GRATITUDE INTO MY HEART NOW
>
> I AM GRATEFUL FOR THIS BEAUTIFUL DAY
>
> I AM THANKFUL FOR EVERYTHING I HAVE
>
> I AM GRATEFUL FOR THE BLESSINGS THIS DAY WILL BRING
>
> I AM GRATEFUL FOR WHO I AM
>
> I AM GRATEFUL TO BE ALIVE
>
> I AM GRATEFUL TO HAVE ALL THE ANSWERS TO MY PROBLEMS

☐ Meditate for five minutes—in a quiet place—on all the things you are grateful for

☐ Do five minutes of stretching

☐ Listen to positive songs

☐ Compliment someone today

DAY 31   DATE: __ / __ / __

EVENING RITUAL

☐ LIST THREE GOOD THINGS THAT HAPPENED TODAY
AND THEN ADD THEM TO THE GRATITUDE JAR.

Circle Three Feelings That Describe Your Mood Today		
Jovial	Hopeful	Bored
Happy	Excited	Creative
Nervous	Neutral	Ambitious
Tired	Depressed	Shy
Stressed	Anxious	Embarrassed
Scattered	Angry	Calm

Describe what brought about these feelings

_____

_____

_____

Who did you compliment today and how did that make you feel?

_____

_____

_____

REFLECTIONS

What makes you feel connected to God/Source Energy/your definition of the Divine?

_____

_____

_____

_____

_____

_____

_____

_____

_____

_____

_____

_____

_____

_____

_____

_____

_____

_____

_____

_____

_____

_____

DAY 32

MORNING RITUAL

Today, I Am Feeling _____.

Today, I Will Accomplish _____.

I Love My _____.

☐ SAY THE FOLLOWING PROMPTS OUT LOUD AND CHECK THE BOX ONCE COMPLETE:

> I INVITE GRATITUDE INTO MY HEART NOW
>
> I AM GRATEFUL FOR THIS BEAUTIFUL DAY
>
> I AM THANKFUL FOR EVERYTHING I HAVE
>
> I AM GRATEFUL FOR THE BLESSINGS THIS DAY WILL BRING
>
> I AM GRATEFUL FOR WHO I AM
>
> I AM GRATEFUL TO BE ALIVE
>
> I AM GRATEFUL TO HAVE ALL THE ANSWERS TO MY PROBLEMS

☐ Meditate for five minutes—in a quiet place—on all the things you are grateful for

☐ Do five minutes of stretching

☐ Listen to positive songs

☐ Compliment someone today

DAY 32

EVENING RITUAL

☐ LIST THREE GOOD THINGS THAT HAPPENED TODAY AND THEN ADD THEM TO THE GRATITUDE JAR.

Circle Three Feelings That Describe Your Mood Today		
Jovial	Hopeful	Bored
Happy	Excited	Creative
Nervous	Neutral	Ambitious
Tired	Depressed	Shy
Stressed	Anxious	Embarrassed
Scattered	Angry	Calm

Describe what brought about these feelings

_____

_____

_____

Who did you compliment today and how did that make you feel?

_____

_____

_____

REFLECTIONS

Name a few things you can easily upgrade and improve that will make you happy.

_____

_____

_____

_____

_____

_____

_____

_____

_____

_____

_____

_____

_____

_____

_____

_____

_____

_____

_____

_____

_____

_____

DAY 33

MORNING RITUAL

Today, I Am Feeling _____.

Today, I Will Accomplish _____.

I Love My _____.

☐ SAY THE FOLLOWING PROMPTS OUT LOUD AND CHECK THE BOX ONCE COMPLETE:

> I INVITE GRATITUDE INTO MY HEART NOW
>
> I AM GRATEFUL FOR THIS BEAUTIFUL DAY
>
> I AM THANKFUL FOR EVERYTHING I HAVE
>
> I AM GRATEFUL FOR THE BLESSINGS THIS DAY WILL BRING
>
> I AM GRATEFUL FOR WHO I AM
>
> I AM GRATEFUL TO BE ALIVE
>
> I AM GRATEFUL TO HAVE ALL THE ANSWERS TO MY PROBLEMS

☐ Meditate for five minutes—in a quiet place—on all the things you are grateful for

☐ Do five minutes of stretching

☐ Listen to positive songs

☐ Compliment someone today

DAY 33

DATE: __ /__ /__

EVENING RITUAL

☐ LIST THREE GOOD THINGS THAT HAPPENED TODAY
AND THEN ADD THEM TO THE GRATITUDE JAR.

Circle Three Feelings That Describe Your Mood Today		
Jovial	Hopeful	Bored
Happy	Excited	Creative
Nervous	Neutral	Ambitious
Tired	Depressed	Shy
Stressed	Anxious	Embarrassed
Scattered	Angry	Calm

Describe what brought about these feelings

_____

_____

_____

Who did you compliment today and how did that make you feel?

_____

_____

_____

REFLECTIONS

Name 10 objects or things around you that you're grateful
for.

_____

_____

_____

_____

_____

_____

_____

_____

_____

_____

_____

_____

_____

_____

_____

_____

_____

_____

_____

_____

_____

_____

DAY 34

MORNING RITUAL

Today, I Am Feeling _____.

Today, I Will Accomplish _____.

I Love My _____.

☐ SAY THE FOLLOWING PROMPTS OUT LOUD AND CHECK THE BOX ONCE COMPLETE:

> I INVITE GRATITUDE INTO MY HEART NOW
>
> I AM GRATEFUL FOR THIS BEAUTIFUL DAY
>
> I AM THANKFUL FOR EVERYTHING I HAVE
>
> I AM GRATEFUL FOR THE BLESSINGS THIS DAY WILL BRING
>
> I AM GRATEFUL FOR WHO I AM
>
> I AM GRATEFUL TO BE ALIVE
>
> I AM GRATEFUL TO HAVE ALL THE ANSWERS TO MY PROBLEMS

☐ Meditate for five minutes—in a quiet place—on all the things you are grateful for

☐ Do five minutes of stretching

☐ Listen to positive songs

☐ Compliment someone today

DAY 34

DATE: __ /__ /__

EVENING RITUAL

☐ LIST THREE GOOD THINGS THAT HAPPENED TODAY
AND THEN ADD THEM TO THE GRATITUDE JAR.

Circle Three Feelings That Describe Your Mood Today		
Jovial	Hopeful	Bored
Happy	Excited	Creative
Nervous	Neutral	Ambitious
Tired	Depressed	Shy
Stressed	Anxious	Embarrassed
Scattered	Angry	Calm

Describe what brought about these feelings

_____

_____

_____

Who did you compliment today and how did that make you feel?

_____

_____

_____

REFLECTIONS

Who are you glad to have met in your life, and how do they add value to it?

_____

_____

_____

_____

_____

_____

_____

_____

_____

_____

_____

_____

_____

_____

_____

_____

_____

_____

_____

_____

_____

_____

"Who does not thank for little
will not thank for much."

-Estonian Proverb

DAY 35

MORNING RITUAL

Today, I Am Feeling _____.
Today, I Will Accomplish _____.
I Love My _____.

☐ SAY THE FOLLOWING PROMPTS OUT LOUD AND CHECK THE BOX ONCE COMPLETE:

> I INVITE GRATITUDE INTO MY HEART NOW
>
> I AM GRATEFUL FOR THIS BEAUTIFUL DAY
>
> I AM THANKFUL FOR EVERYTHING I HAVE
>
> I AM GRATEFUL FOR THE BLESSINGS THIS DAY WILL BRING
>
> I AM GRATEFUL FOR WHO I AM
>
> I AM GRATEFUL TO BE ALIVE
>
> I AM GRATEFUL TO HAVE ALL THE ANSWERS TO MY PROBLEMS

☐ Meditate for five minutes—in a quiet place—on all the things you are grateful for
☐ Do five minutes of stretching
☐ Listen to positive songs
☐ Compliment someone today

DAY 35

EVENING RITUAL

☐ LIST THREE GOOD THINGS THAT HAPPENED TODAY
AND THEN ADD THEM TO THE GRATITUDE JAR.

Circle Three Feelings That Describe Your Mood Today		
Jovial	Hopeful	Bored
Happy	Excited	Creative
Nervous	Neutral	Ambitious
Tired	Depressed	Shy
Stressed	Anxious	Embarrassed
Scattered	Angry	Calm

Describe what brought about these feelings

_____

_____

_____

Who did you compliment today and how did that make you feel?

_____

_____

_____

REFLECTIONS

What household or personal care products bring you joy?

_____

_____

_____

_____

_____

_____

_____

_____

_____

_____

_____

_____

_____

_____

_____

_____

_____

_____

_____

_____

_____

_____

_____

_____

_____

DAY 36

DATE: __ /__ /__

MORNING RITUAL

Today, I Am Feeling _____.

Today, I Will Accomplish _____.

I Love My _____.

☐ SAY THE FOLLOWING PROMPTS OUT LOUD AND CHECK THE BOX ONCE COMPLETE:

I INVITE GRATITUDE INTO MY HEART NOW

I AM GRATEFUL FOR THIS BEAUTIFUL DAY

I AM THANKFUL FOR EVERYTHING I HAVE

I AM GRATEFUL FOR THE BLESSINGS THIS DAY WILL BRING

I AM GRATEFUL FOR WHO I AM

I AM GRATEFUL TO BE ALIVE

I AM GRATEFUL TO HAVE ALL THE ANSWERS TO MY PROBLEMS

☐ Meditate for five minutes—in a quiet place—on all the things you are grateful for

☐ Do five minutes of stretching

☐ Listen to positive songs

☐ Compliment someone today

DAY 36

EVENING RITUAL

"He is a wise man who does not grieve for the things which he has not but rejoices for those which he has."

—Epictetus

Circle Three Feelings That Describe Your Mood Today		
Jovial	Hopeful	Bored
Happy	Excited	Creative
Nervous	Neutral	Ambitious
Tired	Depressed	Shy
Stressed	Anxious	Embarrassed
Scattered	Angry	Calm

Describe what brought about these feelings

_____

_____

_____

Who did you compliment today and how did that make you feel?

_____

_____

_____

REFLECTIONS

Describe a freedom you are grateful for.

_____

_____

_____

_____

_____

_____

_____

_____

_____

_____

_____

_____

_____

_____

_____

_____

_____

_____

_____

_____

_____

_____

_____

DAY 37

MORNING RITUAL

Today, I Am Feeling _____.

Today, I Will Accomplish _____.

I Love My _____.

☐ SAY THE FOLLOWING PROMPTS OUT LOUD AND
CHECK THE BOX ONCE COMPLETE:

> I INVITE GRATITUDE INTO MY HEART NOW
>
> I AM GRATEFUL FOR THIS BEAUTIFUL DAY
>
> I AM THANKFUL FOR EVERYTHING I HAVE
>
> I AM GRATEFUL FOR THE BLESSINGS THIS DAY
> WILL BRING
>
> I AM GRATEFUL FOR WHO I AM
>
> I AM GRATEFUL TO BE ALIVE
>
> I AM GRATEFUL TO HAVE ALL THE ANSWERS
> TO MY PROBLEMS

☐ Meditate for five minutes—in a quiet place—on all the things you
are grateful for

☐ Do five minutes of stretching

☐ Listen to positive songs

☐ Compliment someone today

DAY 37

EVENING RITUAL

☐ LIST THREE GOOD THINGS THAT HAPPENED TODAY AND THEN ADD THEM TO THE GRATITUDE JAR.

Circle Three Feelings That Describe Your Mood Today		
Jovial	Hopeful	Bored
Happy	Excited	Creative
Nervous	Neutral	Ambitious
Tired	Depressed	Shy
Stressed	Anxious	Embarrassed
Scattered	Angry	Calm

Describe what brought about these feelings

_____

_____

_____

Who did you compliment today and how did that make you feel?

_____

_____

_____

REFLECTIONS

The biggest gift in my life right now is:

_____

_____

_____

_____

_____

_____

_____

_____

_____

_____

_____

_____

_____

_____

_____

_____

_____

_____

_____

_____

_____

_____

_____

DAY 38   DATE: __ / __ / __

MORNING RITUAL

Today, I Am Feeling _____.

Today, I Will Accomplish _____.

I Love My _____.

☐ SAY THE FOLLOWING PROMPTS OUT LOUD AND CHECK THE BOX ONCE COMPLETE:

> I INVITE GRATITUDE INTO MY HEART NOW
>
> I AM GRATEFUL FOR THIS BEAUTIFUL DAY
>
> I AM THANKFUL FOR EVERYTHING I HAVE
>
> I AM GRATEFUL FOR THE BLESSINGS THIS DAY WILL BRING
>
> I AM GRATEFUL FOR WHO I AM
>
> I AM GRATEFUL TO BE ALIVE
>
> I AM GRATEFUL TO HAVE ALL THE ANSWERS TO MY PROBLEMS

☐ Meditate for five minutes—in a quiet place—on all the things you are grateful for

☐ Do five minutes of stretching

☐ Listen to positive songs

☐ Compliment someone today

DAY 38

DATE: __ / __ / __

EVENING RITUAL

☐ LIST THREE GOOD THINGS THAT HAPPENED TODAY
AND THEN ADD THEM TO THE GRATITUDE JAR.

Circle Three Feelings That Describe Your Mood Today		
Jovial	Hopeful	Bored
Happy	Excited	Creative
Nervous	Neutral	Ambitious
Tired	Depressed	Shy
Stressed	Anxious	Embarrassed
Scattered	Angry	Calm

Describe what brought about these feelings

_____

_____

_____

Who did you compliment today and how did that make you feel?

_____

_____

_____

REFLECTIONS

Name 5 things you're proud of.

_____

_____

_____

_____

_____

_____

_____

_____

_____

_____

_____

_____

_____

_____

_____

_____

_____

_____

_____

_____

_____

_____

_____

DAY 39

MORNING RITUAL

Today, I Am Feeling _____.

Today, I Will Accomplish _____.

I Love My _____.

☐ SAY THE FOLLOWING PROMPTS OUT LOUD AND CHECK THE BOX ONCE COMPLETE:

> I INVITE GRATITUDE INTO MY HEART NOW
>
> I AM GRATEFUL FOR THIS BEAUTIFUL DAY
>
> I AM THANKFUL FOR EVERYTHING I HAVE
>
> I AM GRATEFUL FOR THE BLESSINGS THIS DAY WILL BRING
>
> I AM GRATEFUL FOR WHO I AM
>
> I AM GRATEFUL TO BE ALIVE
>
> I AM GRATEFUL TO HAVE ALL THE ANSWERS TO MY PROBLEMS

☐ Meditate for five minutes—in a quiet place—on all the things you are grateful for

☐ Do five minutes of stretching

☐ Listen to positive songs

☐ Compliment someone today

DAY 39

DATE: __/__/__

EVENING RITUAL

☐ LIST THREE GOOD THINGS THAT HAPPENED TODAY
AND THEN ADD THEM TO THE GRATITUDE JAR.

Circle Three Feelings That Describe Your Mood Today		
Jovial	Hopeful	Bored
Happy	Excited	Creative
Nervous	Neutral	Ambitious
Tired	Depressed	Shy
Stressed	Anxious	Embarrassed
Scattered	Angry	Calm

Describe what brought about these feelings

_____

_____

_____

Who did you compliment today and how did that make you feel?

_____

_____

_____

REFLECTIONS

Write about a time someone surprised you with politeness, kindness, or grace.

_____
_____
_____
_____
_____
_____
_____
_____
_____
_____
_____
_____
_____
_____
_____
_____
_____
_____
_____
_____
_____
_____
_____
_____
_____
_____

DAY 40   DATE: __ / __ / __

MORNING RITUAL

Today, I Am Feeling _____.

Today, I Will Accomplish _____.

I Love My _____.

☐ SAY THE FOLLOWING PROMPTS OUT LOUD AND CHECK THE BOX ONCE COMPLETE:

> I INVITE GRATITUDE INTO MY HEART NOW
>
> I AM GRATEFUL FOR THIS BEAUTIFUL DAY
>
> I AM THANKFUL FOR EVERYTHING I HAVE
>
> I AM GRATEFUL FOR THE BLESSINGS THIS DAY WILL BRING
>
> I AM GRATEFUL FOR WHO I AM
>
> I AM GRATEFUL TO BE ALIVE
>
> I AM GRATEFUL TO HAVE ALL THE ANSWERS TO MY PROBLEMS

☐ Meditate for five minutes—in a quiet place—on all the things you are grateful for

☐ Do five minutes of stretching

☐ Listen to positive songs

☐ Compliment someone today

DAY 40

DATE: __ /__ /__

EVENING RITUAL

☐ LIST THREE GOOD THINGS THAT HAPPENED TODAY
AND THEN ADD THEM TO THE GRATITUDE JAR.

Circle Three Feelings That Describe Your Mood Today		
Jovial	Hopeful	Bored
Happy	Excited	Creative
Nervous	Neutral	Ambitious
Tired	Depressed	Shy
Stressed	Anxious	Embarrassed
Scattered	Angry	Calm

Describe what brought about these feelings

_____

_____

_____

Who did you compliment today and how did that make you feel?

_____

_____

_____

REFLECTIONS

What are the positive aspects of your job?

_____

_____

_____

_____

_____

_____

_____

_____

_____

_____

_____

_____

_____

_____

_____

_____

_____

_____

_____

_____

_____

_____

_____

DAY 41 DATE: __ / __ / __

MORNING RITUAL

Today, I Am Feeling _____.
Today, I Will Accomplish _____.
I Love My _____.

☐ SAY THE FOLLOWING PROMPTS OUT LOUD AND
   CHECK THE BOX ONCE COMPLETE:

> I INVITE GRATITUDE INTO MY HEART NOW
>
> I AM GRATEFUL FOR THIS BEAUTIFUL DAY
>
> I AM THANKFUL FOR EVERYTHING I HAVE
>
> I AM GRATEFUL FOR THE BLESSINGS THIS DAY
> WILL BRING
>
> I AM GRATEFUL FOR WHO I AM
>
> I AM GRATEFUL TO BE ALIVE
>
> I AM GRATEFUL TO HAVE ALL THE ANSWERS
> TO MY PROBLEMS

☐ Meditate for five minutes—in a quiet place—on all the things you
   are grateful for
☐ Do five minutes of stretching
☐ Listen to positive songs
☐ Compliment someone today

DAY 41

EVENING RITUAL

☐ LIST THREE GOOD THINGS THAT HAPPENED TODAY
AND THEN ADD THEM TO THE GRATITUDE JAR.

Circle Three Feelings That Describe Your Mood Today		
Jovial	Hopeful	Bored
Happy	Excited	Creative
Nervous	Neutral	Ambitious
Tired	Depressed	Shy
Stressed	Anxious	Embarrassed
Scattered	Angry	Calm

Describe what brought about these feelings

_____

_____

_____

Who did you compliment today and how did that make you feel?

_____

_____

_____

Take 5 strips out of your gratitude jar and list them below

_____

_____

_____

Exercise

Think about a person who has recently done something good for you, to whom you have not yet expressed your gratitude. This person may be a friend, family member, coworker, teacher, or mentor.

Next, write them an email or letter. Use these guidelines to write an effective and grateful letter:

☐ Write as though you are addressing the person directly.
☐ Describe what this person has done that makes you grateful, and how they have impacted your life. Be as concrete as possible here.
☐ Describe what you are doing in life now, and how frequently you remember their act of kindness or generosity.
☐ Try to keep your letter to about 300 words or so.

Who are you addressing this letter to and why?

_____

_____

_____

_____

_____

_____

_____

_____

_____

_____

_____

_____

_____

_____

_____

_____

"Gratitude opens the door to the power, the wisdom, the creativity of the universe. You open the door through gratitude."

- Deepak Chopra

DAY 42

DATE: __ / __ / __

MORNING RITUAL

Today, I Am Feeling _____.

Today, I Will Accomplish _____.

I Love My _____.

☐ SAY THE FOLLOWING PROMPTS OUT LOUD AND CHECK THE BOX ONCE COMPLETE:

> I INVITE GRATITUDE INTO MY HEART NOW
>
> I AM GRATEFUL FOR THIS BEAUTIFUL DAY
>
> I AM THANKFUL FOR EVERYTHING I HAVE
>
> I AM GRATEFUL FOR THE BLESSINGS THIS DAY WILL BRING
>
> I AM GRATEFUL FOR WHO I AM
>
> I AM GRATEFUL TO BE ALIVE
>
> I AM GRATEFUL TO HAVE ALL THE ANSWERS TO MY PROBLEMS

☐ Meditate for five minutes—in a quiet place—on all the things you are grateful for

☐ Do five minutes of stretching

☐ Listen to positive songs

☐ Compliment someone today

DAY 42

EVENING RITUAL

☐ LIST THREE GOOD THINGS THAT HAPPENED TODAY
AND THEN ADD THEM TO THE GRATITUDE JAR.

Circle Three Feelings That Describe Your Mood Today

Jovial	Hopeful	Bored
Happy	Excited	Creative
Nervous	Neutral	Ambitious
Tired	Depressed	Shy
Stressed	Anxious	Embarrassed
Scattered	Angry	Calm

Describe what brought about these feelings

_____

_____

_____

Who did you compliment today and how did that make you feel?

_____

_____

_____

EXERCISE

1. Thank you _____ for _____.

2. Thank yourself for _____.

3. Thank your God/Universe for _____.

4. I am blessed for _____ and _____.

5. I am beautiful and _____.

6. I am grateful most for _____ and _____.

DAY 43

MORNING RITUAL

Today, I Am Feeling _____.

Today, I Will Accomplish _____.

I Love My _____.

☐ SAY THE FOLLOWING PROMPTS OUT LOUD AND CHECK THE BOX ONCE COMPLETE:

> I INVITE GRATITUDE INTO MY HEART NOW
>
> I AM GRATEFUL FOR THIS BEAUTIFUL DAY
>
> I AM THANKFUL FOR EVERYTHING I HAVE
>
> I AM GRATEFUL FOR THE BLESSINGS THIS DAY WILL BRING
>
> I AM GRATEFUL FOR WHO I AM
>
> I AM GRATEFUL TO BE ALIVE
>
> I AM GRATEFUL TO HAVE ALL THE ANSWERS TO MY PROBLEMS

☐ Meditate for five minutes—in a quiet place—on all the things you are grateful for

☐ Do five minutes of stretching

☐ Listen to positive songs

☐ Compliment someone today

DAY 43

EVENING RITUAL

☐ LIST THREE GOOD THINGS THAT HAPPENED TODAY
AND THEN ADD THEM TO THE GRATITUDE JAR.

Circle Three Feelings That Describe Your Mood Today		
Jovial	Hopeful	Bored
Happy	Excited	Creative
Nervous	Neutral	Ambitious
Tired	Depressed	Shy
Stressed	Anxious	Embarrassed
Scattered	Angry	Calm

Describe what brought about these feelings

_____

_____

_____

Who did you compliment today and how did that make you feel?

_____

_____

_____

REFLECTIONS

Document all of your most treasured memories throughout your childhood

_____

_____

_____

_____

_____

_____

_____

_____

_____

_____

_____

_____

_____

_____

_____

_____

_____

_____

_____

_____

_____

_____

_____

_____

_____

DAY 44

MORNING RITUAL

Today, I Am Feeling _____.

Today, I Will Accomplish _____.

I Love My _____.

☐ SAY THE FOLLOWING PROMPTS OUT LOUD AND CHECK THE BOX ONCE COMPLETE:

> I INVITE GRATITUDE INTO MY HEART NOW
>
> I AM GRATEFUL FOR THIS BEAUTIFUL DAY
>
> I AM THANKFUL FOR EVERYTHING I HAVE
>
> I AM GRATEFUL FOR THE BLESSINGS THIS DAY WILL BRING
>
> I AM GRATEFUL FOR WHO I AM
>
> I AM GRATEFUL TO BE ALIVE
>
> I AM GRATEFUL TO HAVE ALL THE ANSWERS TO MY PROBLEMS

☐ Meditate for five minutes—in a quiet place—on all the things you are grateful for

☐ Do five minutes of stretching

☐ Listen to positive songs

☐ Compliment someone today

DAY 44

EVENING RITUAL

☐ LIST THREE GOOD THINGS THAT HAPPENED TODAY
AND THEN ADD THEM TO THE GRATITUDE JAR.

Circle Three Feelings That Describe Your Mood Today

Jovial	Hopeful	Bored
Happy	Excited	Creative
Nervous	Neutral	Ambitious
Tired	Depressed	Shy
Stressed	Anxious	Embarrassed
Scattered	Angry	Calm

Describe what brought about these feelings

_____

_____

_____

Who did you compliment today and how did that make you feel?

_____

_____

_____

REFLECTIONS

What good is currently happening in the world and how does it affect you?

_____

_____

_____

_____

_____

_____

_____

_____

_____

_____

_____

_____

_____

_____

_____

_____

_____

_____

_____

_____

_____

_____

_____

DAY 45

DATE: __ / __ / __

MORNING RITUAL

Today, I Am Feeling _____.

Today, I Will Accomplish _____.

I Love My _____.

☐ SAY THE FOLLOWING PROMPTS OUT LOUD AND CHECK THE BOX ONCE COMPLETE:

> I INVITE GRATITUDE INTO MY HEART NOW
>
> I AM GRATEFUL FOR THIS BEAUTIFUL DAY
>
> I AM THANKFUL FOR EVERYTHING I HAVE
>
> I AM GRATEFUL FOR THE BLESSINGS THIS DAY WILL BRING
>
> I AM GRATEFUL FOR WHO I AM
>
> I AM GRATEFUL TO BE ALIVE
>
> I AM GRATEFUL TO HAVE ALL THE ANSWERS TO MY PROBLEMS

☐ Meditate for five minutes—in a quiet place—on all the things you are grateful for

☐ Do five minutes of stretching

☐ Listen to positive songs

☐ Compliment someone today

DAY 45 DATE: __ /__ /__

EVENING RITUAL

☐ LIST THREE GOOD THINGS THAT HAPPENED TODAY AND THEN ADD THEM TO THE GRATITUDE JAR.

Circle Three Feelings That Describe Your Mood Today

Jovial	Hopeful	Bored
Happy	Excited	Creative
Nervous	Neutral	Ambitious
Tired	Depressed	Shy
Stressed	Anxious	Embarrassed
Scattered	Angry	Calm

Describe what brought about these feelings

_____

_____

_____

Who did you compliment today and how did that make you feel?

_____

_____

_____

REFLECTIONS

Write about a hidden blessing in a difficult situation.

DAY 46

MORNING RITUAL

Today, I Am Feeling _____.

Today, I Will Accomplish _____.

I Love My _____.

☐ SAY THE FOLLOWING PROMPTS OUT LOUD AND CHECK THE BOX ONCE COMPLETE:

> I INVITE GRATITUDE INTO MY HEART NOW
>
> I AM GRATEFUL FOR THIS BEAUTIFUL DAY
>
> I AM THANKFUL FOR EVERYTHING I HAVE
>
> I AM GRATEFUL FOR THE BLESSINGS THIS DAY WILL BRING
>
> I AM GRATEFUL FOR WHO I AM
>
> I AM GRATEFUL TO BE ALIVE
>
> I AM GRATEFUL TO HAVE ALL THE ANSWERS TO MY PROBLEMS

☐ Meditate for five minutes—in a quiet place—on all the things you are grateful for

☐ Do five minutes of stretching

☐ Listen to positive songs

☐ Compliment someone today

DAY 46

EVENING RITUAL

☐ LIST THREE GOOD THINGS THAT HAPPENED TODAY
AND THEN ADD THEM TO THE GRATITUDE JAR.

Circle Three Feelings That Describe Your Mood Today		
Jovial	Hopeful	Bored
Happy	Excited	Creative
Nervous	Neutral	Ambitious
Tired	Depressed	Shy
Stressed	Anxious	Embarrassed
Scattered	Angry	Calm

Describe what brought about these feelings

_____

_____

_____

Who did you compliment today and how did that make you feel?

_____

_____

_____

REFLECTIONS

List 3 things that make you feel strong and why?

_____

_____

_____

_____

_____

_____

_____

_____

_____

_____

_____

_____

_____

_____

_____

_____

_____

_____

_____

_____

_____

_____

_____

_____

_____

DAY 47

MORNING RITUAL

Today, I Am Feeling _____.

Today, I Will Accomplish _____.

I Love My _____.

☐ SAY THE FOLLOWING PROMPTS OUT LOUD AND CHECK THE BOX ONCE COMPLETE:

> I INVITE GRATITUDE INTO MY HEART NOW
>
> I AM GRATEFUL FOR THIS BEAUTIFUL DAY
>
> I AM THANKFUL FOR EVERYTHING I HAVE
>
> I AM GRATEFUL FOR THE BLESSINGS THIS DAY WILL BRING
>
> I AM GRATEFUL FOR WHO I AM
>
> I AM GRATEFUL TO BE ALIVE
>
> I AM GRATEFUL TO HAVE ALL THE ANSWERS TO MY PROBLEMS

☐ Meditate for five minutes—in a quiet place—on all the things you are grateful for

☐ Do five minutes of stretching

☐ Listen to positive songs

☐ Compliment someone today

DAY 47

EVENING RITUAL

☐ LIST THREE GOOD THINGS THAT HAPPENED TODAY
AND THEN ADD THEM TO THE GRATITUDE JAR.

Circle Three Feelings That Describe Your Mood Today		
Jovial	Hopeful	Bored
Happy	Excited	Creative
Nervous	Neutral	Ambitious
Tired	Depressed	Shy
Stressed	Anxious	Embarrassed
Scattered	Angry	Calm

Describe what brought about these feelings

_____

_____

_____

Who did you compliment today and how did that make you feel?

_____

_____

_____

REFLECTIONS

List the hobbies and pastimes you're most grateful for in life.

_____

_____

_____

_____

_____

_____

_____

_____

_____

_____

_____

_____

_____

_____

_____

_____

_____

_____

_____

_____

_____

_____

_____

DAY 48

MORNING RITUAL

Today, I Am Feeling _____.

Today, I Will Accomplish _____.

I Love My _____.

☐ SAY THE FOLLOWING PROMPTS OUT LOUD AND CHECK THE BOX ONCE COMPLETE:

> I INVITE GRATITUDE INTO MY HEART NOW
>
> I AM GRATEFUL FOR THIS BEAUTIFUL DAY
>
> I AM THANKFUL FOR EVERYTHING I HAVE
>
> I AM GRATEFUL FOR THE BLESSINGS THIS DAY WILL BRING
>
> I AM GRATEFUL FOR WHO I AM
>
> I AM GRATEFUL TO BE ALIVE
>
> I AM GRATEFUL TO HAVE ALL THE ANSWERS TO MY PROBLEMS

☐ Meditate for five minutes—in a quiet place—on all the things you are grateful for

☐ Do five minutes of stretching

☐ Listen to positive songs

☐ Compliment someone today

DAY 48

EVENING RITUAL

☐ LIST THREE GOOD THINGS THAT HAPPENED TODAY
AND THEN ADD THEM TO THE GRATITUDE JAR.

Circle Three Feelings That Describe Your Mood Today		
Jovial	Hopeful	Bored
Happy	Excited	Creative
Nervous	Neutral	Ambitious
Tired	Depressed	Shy
Stressed	Anxious	Embarrassed
Scattered	Angry	Calm

Describe what brought about these feelings

_____

_____

_____

Who did you compliment today and how did that make you feel?

_____

_____

_____

REFLECTIONS

What kind of things do you love to learn and why? What would you like to learn next, and why would it add value to your life?

_____

_____

_____

_____

_____

_____

_____

_____

_____

_____

_____

_____

_____

_____

_____

_____

_____

_____

_____

_____

Offer thanks in all situations –
especially in difficulties

–1 Thessalonians 5:18)

DAY 49

MORNING RITUAL

Today, I Am Feeling _____.

Today, I Will Accomplish _____.

I Love My _____.

☐ SAY THE FOLLOWING PROMPTS OUT LOUD AND CHECK THE BOX ONCE COMPLETE:

> I INVITE GRATITUDE INTO MY HEART NOW
>
> I AM GRATEFUL FOR THIS BEAUTIFUL DAY
>
> I AM THANKFUL FOR EVERYTHING I HAVE
>
> I AM GRATEFUL FOR THE BLESSINGS THIS DAY WILL BRING
>
> I AM GRATEFUL FOR WHO I AM
>
> I AM GRATEFUL TO BE ALIVE
>
> I AM GRATEFUL TO HAVE ALL THE ANSWERS TO MY PROBLEMS

☐ Meditate for five minutes—in a quiet place—on all the things you are grateful for

☐ Do five minutes of stretching

☐ Listen to positive songs

☐ Compliment someone today

DAY 49

EVENING RITUAL

☐ LIST THREE GOOD THINGS THAT HAPPENED TODAY
AND THEN ADD THEM TO THE GRATITUDE JAR.

Circle Three Feelings That Describe Your Mood Today		
Jovial	Hopeful	Bored
Happy	Excited	Creative
Nervous	Neutral	Ambitious
Tired	Depressed	Shy
Stressed	Anxious	Embarrassed
Scattered	Angry	Calm

Describe what brought about these feelings

_____

_____

_____

Who did you compliment today and how did that make you feel?

_____

_____

_____

REFLECTIONS

What's the best piece of advice you have ever been given and why?

_____

_____

_____

_____

_____

_____

_____

_____

_____

_____

_____

_____

_____

_____

_____

_____

_____

_____

_____

_____

_____

_____

_____

_____

_____

DAY 50

DATE: __ / __ / __

MORNING RITUAL

Today, I Am Feeling _____.

Today, I Will Accomplish _____.

I Love My _____.

☐ SAY THE FOLLOWING PROMPTS OUT LOUD AND CHECK THE BOX ONCE COMPLETE:

> I INVITE GRATITUDE INTO MY HEART NOW
>
> I AM GRATEFUL FOR THIS BEAUTIFUL DAY
>
> I AM THANKFUL FOR EVERYTHING I HAVE
>
> I AM GRATEFUL FOR THE BLESSINGS THIS DAY WILL BRING
>
> I AM GRATEFUL FOR WHO I AM
>
> I AM GRATEFUL TO BE ALIVE
>
> I AM GRATEFUL TO HAVE ALL THE ANSWERS TO MY PROBLEMS

☐ Meditate for five minutes—in a quiet place—on all the things you are grateful for

☐ Do five minutes of stretching

☐ Listen to positive songs

☐ Compliment someone today

DAY 50   DATE: __ / __ / __

EVENING RITUAL

☐ LIST THREE GOOD THINGS THAT HAPPENED TODAY AND THEN ADD THEM TO THE GRATITUDE JAR.

Circle Three Feelings That Describe Your Mood Today		
Jovial	Hopeful	Bored
Happy	Excited	Creative
Nervous	Neutral	Ambitious
Tired	Depressed	Shy
Stressed	Anxious	Embarrassed
Scattered	Angry	Calm

Describe what brought about these feelings

_____

_____

_____

Who did you compliment today and how did that make you feel?

_____

_____

_____

Activity

Think about an undesirable circumstance in your life and ask yourself the following questions:

What's good about this?

_____

_____

_____

What can I learn from this?

_____

_____

_____

How can I benefit from this?

_____

_____

_____

Is there something about this situation that I can be grateful for?

_____

_____

_____

DAY 51

DATE: __ /__ /__

MORNING RITUAL

Today, I Am Feeling _____.

Today, I Will Accomplish _____.

I Love My _____.

☐ SAY THE FOLLOWING PROMPTS OUT LOUD AND CHECK THE BOX ONCE COMPLETE:

> I INVITE GRATITUDE INTO MY HEART NOW
>
> I AM GRATEFUL FOR THIS BEAUTIFUL DAY
>
> I AM THANKFUL FOR EVERYTHING I HAVE
>
> I AM GRATEFUL FOR THE BLESSINGS THIS DAY WILL BRING
>
> I AM GRATEFUL FOR WHO I AM
>
> I AM GRATEFUL TO BE ALIVE
>
> I AM GRATEFUL TO HAVE ALL THE ANSWERS TO MY PROBLEMS

☐ Meditate for five minutes—in a quiet place—on all the things you are grateful for

☐ Do five minutes of stretching

☐ Listen to positive songs

☐ Compliment someone today

DAY 51

EVENING RITUAL

☐ LIST THREE GOOD THINGS THAT HAPPENED TODAY AND THEN ADD THEM TO THE GRATITUDE JAR.

Circle Three Feelings That Describe Your Mood Today		
Jovial	Hopeful	Bored
Happy	Excited	Creative
Nervous	Neutral	Ambitious
Tired	Depressed	Shy
Stressed	Anxious	Embarrassed
Scattered	Angry	Calm

Describe what brought about these feelings

_____

_____

_____

Who did you compliment today and how did that make you feel?

_____

_____

_____

Take five strips out of your gratitude jar and list them here

_____

_____

_____

ACTIVITY

Complete these sentences.

1. Tomorrow, I will focus on

_____

_____

_____

2. Tomorrow, I will succeed at

_____

_____

_____

3. Today, I release

_____

_____

_____

4. I will prosper in

_____

_____

_____

5. I will win favor with

_____

_____

_____

6. Today, I forgive _____ for _____.

7. This week, I will treat myself to

_____

_____

_____

DAY 52　　　　　DATE: __ / __ / __

MORNING RITUAL

Today, I Am Feeling _____.
Today, I Will Accomplish _____.
I Love My _____.

☐ SAY THE FOLLOWING PROMPTS OUT LOUD AND CHECK THE BOX ONCE COMPLETE:

I INVITE GRATITUDE INTO MY HEART NOW

I AM GRATEFUL FOR THIS BEAUTIFUL DAY

I AM THANKFUL FOR EVERYTHING I HAVE

I AM GRATEFUL FOR THE BLESSINGS THIS DAY WILL BRING

I AM GRATEFUL FOR WHO I AM

I AM GRATEFUL TO BE ALIVE

I AM GRATEFUL TO HAVE ALL THE ANSWERS TO MY PROBLEMS

☐ Meditate for five minutes—in a quiet place—on all the things you are grateful for
☐ Do five minutes of stretching
☐ Listen to positive songs
☐ Compliment someone today

DAY 52

EVENING RITUAL

☐ LIST THREE GOOD THINGS THAT HAPPENED TODAY
AND THEN ADD THEM TO THE GRATITUDE JAR.

Circle Three Feelings That Describe Your Mood Today		
Jovial	Hopeful	Bored
Happy	Excited	Creative
Nervous	Neutral	Ambitious
Tired	Depressed	Shy
Stressed	Anxious	Embarrassed
Scattered	Angry	Calm

Describe what brought about these feelings

_____

_____

_____

Who did you compliment today and how did that make you feel?

_____

_____

_____

REFLECTIONS

List the things that you think you *should* be doing in life, but you are not doing yet and why.

_____

_____

_____

_____

_____

_____

_____

_____

_____

_____

_____

_____

_____

_____

_____

_____

_____

_____

_____

_____

_____

_____

_____

_____

_____

DAY 53

DATE: __ /__ /__

MORNING RITUAL

Today, I Am Feeling _____.

Today, I Will Accomplish _____.

I Love My _____.

☐ SAY THE FOLLOWING PROMPTS OUT LOUD AND CHECK THE BOX ONCE COMPLETE:

> I INVITE GRATITUDE INTO MY HEART NOW
>
> I AM GRATEFUL FOR THIS BEAUTIFUL DAY
>
> I AM THANKFUL FOR EVERYTHING I HAVE
>
> I AM GRATEFUL FOR THE BLESSINGS THIS DAY WILL BRING
>
> I AM GRATEFUL FOR WHO I AM
>
> I AM GRATEFUL TO BE ALIVE
>
> I AM GRATEFUL TO HAVE ALL THE ANSWERS TO MY PROBLEMS

☐ Meditate for five minutes—in a quiet place—on all the things you are grateful for

☐ Do five minutes of stretching

☐ Listen to positive songs

☐ Compliment someone today

DAY 53

DATE: __ / __ / __

EVENING RITUAL

☐ LIST THREE GOOD THINGS THAT HAPPENED TODAY AND THEN ADD THEM TO THE GRATITUDE JAR.

Circle Three Feelings That Describe Your Mood Today

Jovial	Hopeful	Bored
Happy	Excited	Creative
Nervous	Neutral	Ambitious
Tired	Depressed	Shy
Stressed	Anxious	Embarrassed
Scattered	Angry	Calm

Describe what brought about these feelings

_____

_____

_____

Who did you compliment today and how did that make you feel?

_____

_____

_____

REFLECTIONS

List the things that you *should not* be doing in life, but you are already doing and why.

_____

_____

_____

_____

_____

_____

_____

_____

_____

_____

_____

_____

_____

_____

_____

_____

_____

_____

_____

_____

_____

_____

_____

DAY 54

MORNING RITUAL

Today, I Am Feeling _____.

Today, I Will Accomplish _____.

I Love My _____.

☐ SAY THE FOLLOWING PROMPTS OUT LOUD AND CHECK THE BOX ONCE COMPLETE:

> I INVITE GRATITUDE INTO MY HEART NOW
>
> I AM GRATEFUL FOR THIS BEAUTIFUL DAY
>
> I AM THANKFUL FOR EVERYTHING I HAVE
>
> I AM GRATEFUL FOR THE BLESSINGS THIS DAY WILL BRING
>
> I AM GRATEFUL FOR WHO I AM
>
> I AM GRATEFUL TO BE ALIVE
>
> I AM GRATEFUL TO HAVE ALL THE ANSWERS TO MY PROBLEMS

☐ Meditate for five minutes—in a quiet place—on all the things you are grateful for

☐ Do five minutes of stretching

☐ Listen positive songs

☐ Compliment someone today

DAY 54

EVENING RITUAL

☐ LIST THREE GOOD THINGS THAT HAPPENED TODAY
  AND THEN ADD THEM TO THE GRATITUDE JAR.

Circle Three Feelings That Describe Your Mood Today		
Jovial	Hopeful	Bored
Happy	Excited	Creative
Nervous	Neutral	Ambitious
Tired	Depressed	Shy
Stressed	Anxious	Embarrassed
Scattered	Angry	Calm

Describe what brought about these feelings

_____

_____

_____

Who did you compliment today and how did that make you feel?

_____

_____

_____

Activity: Complete these sentences:

The last person that gave me a gift was

_____

_____

_____

The best gift I ever received was

_____

_____

_____

The best thing that ever happened to me was

_____

_____

_____

I love _____ because

_____

_____

_____

I am grateful for _____ because

_____

_____

_____

_____ makes me feel loved because

_____

_____

_____

DAY 55

MORNING RITUAL

Today, I Am Feeling _____.

Today, I Will Accomplish _____.

I Love My _____.

☐ SAY THE FOLLOWING PROMPTS OUT LOUD AND
CHECK THE BOX ONCE COMPLETE:

> I INVITE GRATITUDE INTO MY HEART NOW
>
> I AM GRATEFUL FOR THIS BEAUTIFUL DAY
>
> I AM THANKFUL FOR EVERYTHING I HAVE
>
> I AM GRATEFUL FOR THE BLESSINGS THIS DAY
> WILL BRING
>
> I AM GRATEFUL FOR WHO I AM
>
> I AM GRATEFUL TO BE ALIVE
>
> I AM GRATEFUL TO HAVE ALL THE ANSWERS
> TO MY PROBLEMS

☐ Meditate for five minutes—in a quiet place—on all the things you
are grateful for

☐ Do five minutes of stretching

☐ Listen to positive songs

☐ Compliment someone today

DAY 55

EVENING RITUAL

☐ LIST THREE GOOD THINGS THAT HAPPENED TODAY AND THEN ADD THEM TO THE GRATITUDE JAR.

Circle Three Feelings That Describe Your Mood Today		
Jovial	Hopeful	Bored
Happy	Excited	Creative
Nervous	Neutral	Ambitious
Tired	Depressed	Shy
Stressed	Anxious	Embarrassed
Scattered	Angry	Calm

Describe what brought about these feelings

_____

_____

_____

Who did you compliment today and how did that make you feel?

_____

_____

_____

REFLECTIONS

List three things you take for granted. Explain why?

_____

_____

_____

_____

_____

_____

_____

_____

_____

_____

_____

_____

_____

_____

_____

_____

_____

_____

_____

_____

_____

_____

"When you are grateful, fear disappears and abundance appears."

–Anthony Robbins

DAY 56

DATE: __ /__ /__

MORNING RITUAL

Today, I Am Feeling _____.
Today, I Will Accomplish _____.
I Love My _____.

☐ SAY THE FOLLOWING PROMPTS OUT LOUD AND CHECK THE BOX ONCE COMPLETE:

> I INVITE GRATITUDE INTO MY HEART NOW
>
> I AM GRATEFUL FOR THIS BEAUTIFUL DAY
>
> I AM THANKFUL FOR EVERYTHING I HAVE
>
> I AM GRATEFUL FOR THE BLESSINGS THIS DAY WILL BRING
>
> I AM GRATEFUL FOR WHO I AM
>
> I AM GRATEFUL TO BE ALIVE
>
> I AM GRATEFUL TO HAVE ALL THE ANSWERS TO MY PROBLEMS

☐ Meditate for five minutes—in a quiet place—on all the things you are grateful for
☐ Do five minutes of stretching
☐ Listen to positive songs
☐ Compliment someone today

DAY 56

EVENING RITUAL

☐ LIST THREE GOOD THINGS THAT HAPPENED TODAY
AND THEN ADD THEM TO THE GRATITUDE JAR.

Circle Three Feelings That Describe Your Mood Today		
Jovial	Hopeful	Bored
Happy	Excited	Creative
Nervous	Neutral	Ambitious
Tired	Depressed	Shy
Stressed	Anxious	Embarrassed
Scattered	Angry	Calm

Describe what brought about these feelings

_____

_____

_____

Who did you compliment today and how did that make you feel?

_____

_____

_____

REFLECTIONS

What is something hard that you do, and it makes you stronger?

_____

_____

_____

_____

_____

_____

_____

_____

_____

_____

_____

_____

_____

_____

_____

_____

_____

_____

_____

_____

_____

_____

_____

DAY 57

DATE: __ / __ / __

MORNING RITUAL

Today, I Am Feeling _____.
Today, I Will Accomplish _____.
I Love My _____.

☐ SAY THE FOLLOWING PROMPTS OUT LOUD AND
CHECK THE BOX ONCE COMPLETE:

> I INVITE GRATITUDE INTO MY HEART NOW
>
> I AM GRATEFUL FOR THIS BEAUTIFUL DAY
>
> I AM THANKFUL FOR EVERYTHING I HAVE
>
> I AM GRATEFUL FOR THE BLESSINGS THIS DAY
> WILL BRING
>
> I AM GRATEFUL FOR WHO I AM
>
> I AM GRATEFUL TO BE ALIVE
>
> I AM GRATEFUL TO HAVE ALL THE ANSWERS
> TO MY PROBLEMS

☐ Meditate for five minutes—in a quiet place—on all the things you
are grateful for
☐ Do five minutes of stretching
☐ Listen to positive songs
☐ Compliment someone today

DAY 57

DATE: __ /__ /__

EVENING RITUAL

☐ LIST THREE GOOD THINGS THAT HAPPENED TODAY
AND THEN ADD THEM TO THE GRATITUDE JAR.

Circle Three Feelings That Describe Your Mood Today		
Jovial	Hopeful	Bored
Happy	Excited	Creative
Nervous	Neutral	Ambitious
Tired	Depressed	Shy
Stressed	Anxious	Embarrassed
Scattered	Angry	Calm

Describe what brought about these feelings

_____

_____

_____

Who did you compliment today and how did that make you feel?

_____

_____

_____

REFLECTIONS

What do you love about your body?

_____

_____

_____

What are your top 3 qualities?

_____

_____

_____

What makes you smile?

_____

_____

_____

Who was the last person that made you laugh?

_____

_____

_____

DAY 58

MORNING RITUAL

Today, I Am Feeling _____.

Today, I Will Accomplish _____.

I Love My _____.

☐ SAY THE FOLLOWING PROMPTS OUT LOUD AND CHECK THE BOX ONCE COMPLETE:

> I INVITE GRATITUDE INTO MY HEART NOW
>
> I AM GRATEFUL FOR THIS BEAUTIFUL DAY
>
> I AM THANKFUL FOR EVERYTHING I HAVE
>
> I AM GRATEFUL FOR THE BLESSINGS THIS DAY WILL BRING
>
> I AM GRATEFUL FOR WHO I AM
>
> I AM GRATEFUL TO BE ALIVE
>
> I AM GRATEFUL TO HAVE ALL THE ANSWERS TO MY PROBLEMS

☐ Meditate for five minutes—in a quiet place—on all the things you are grateful for

☐ Do five minutes of stretching

☐ Listen to positive songs

☐ Compliment someone today

DAY 58

EVENING RITUAL

☐ LIST THREE GOOD THINGS THAT HAPPENED TODAY
AND THEN ADD THEM TO THE GRATITUDE JAR.

Circle Three Feelings That Describe Your Mood Today		
Jovial	Hopeful	Bored
Happy	Excited	Creative
Nervous	Neutral	Ambitious
Tired	Depressed	Shy
Stressed	Anxious	Embarrassed
Scattered	Angry	Calm

Describe what brought about these feelings

_____

_____

_____

Who did you compliment today and how did that make you feel?

_____

_____

_____

REFLECTIONS

Describe a time that God/the Universe provided for you when you were worried.

_____

_____

_____

_____

_____

_____

_____

_____

_____

_____

_____

_____

_____

_____

_____

_____

_____

_____

_____

_____

_____

_____

_____

_____

_____

DAY 59

MORNING RITUAL

Today, I Am Feeling _____.

Today, I Will Accomplish _____.

I Love My _____.

☐ SAY THE FOLLOWING PROMPTS OUT LOUD AND CHECK THE BOX ONCE COMPLETE:

> I INVITE GRATITUDE INTO MY HEART NOW
>
> I AM GRATEFUL FOR THIS BEAUTIFUL DAY
>
> I AM THANKFUL FOR EVERYTHING I HAVE
>
> I AM GRATEFUL FOR THE BLESSINGS THIS DAY WILL BRING
>
> I AM GRATEFUL FOR WHO I AM
>
> I AM GRATEFUL TO BE ALIVE
>
> I AM GRATEFUL TO HAVE ALL THE ANSWERS TO MY PROBLEMS

☐ Meditate for five minutes—in a quiet place—on all the things you are grateful for

☐ Do five minutes of stretching

☐ Listen to positive songs

☐ Compliment someone today

DAY 59

EVENING RITUAL

☐ LIST THREE GOOD THINGS THAT HAPPENED TODAY
AND THEN ADD THEM TO THE GRATITUDE JAR.

Circle Three Feelings That Describe Your Mood Today		
Jovial	Hopeful	Bored
Happy	Excited	Creative
Nervous	Neutral	Ambitious
Tired	Depressed	Shy
Stressed	Anxious	Embarrassed
Scattered	Angry	Calm

Describe what brought about these feelings

_____

_____

_____

Who did you compliment today and how did that make you feel?

_____

_____

_____

REFLECTIONS

Write a letter to your future self, detailing all of the goodness in your life and the things you have achieved.

DAY 60

MORNING RITUAL

Today, I Am Feeling _____.
Today, I Will Accomplish _____.
I Love My _____.

☐ SAY THE FOLLOWING PROMPTS OUT LOUD AND
CHECK THE BOX ONCE COMPLETE:

> I INVITE GRATITUDE INTO MY HEART NOW
>
> I AM GRATEFUL FOR THIS BEAUTIFUL DAY
>
> I AM THANKFUL FOR EVERYTHING I HAVE
>
> I AM GRATEFUL FOR THE BLESSINGS THIS DAY
> WILL BRING
>
> I AM GRATEFUL FOR WHO I AM
>
> I AM GRATEFUL TO BE ALIVE
>
> I AM GRATEFUL TO HAVE ALL THE ANSWERS
> TO MY PROBLEMS

☐ Meditate for five minutes—in a quiet place—on all the things you
  are grateful for
☐ Do five minutes of stretching
☐ Listen to positive songs
☐ Compliment someone today

How grateful are you feeling right now? Circle one.

1-Not grateful at all   *2-Not grateful enough*   *3. Extremely grateful*

Has the number changed in the last 60 days? If so, how?

_____

_____

DAY 60

DATE: __ /__ /__

EVENING RITUAL

☐ LIST THREE GOOD THINGS THAT HAPPENED TODAY
AND THEN ADD THEM TO THE GRATITUDE JAR.

Circle Three Feelings That Describe Your Mood Today		
Jovial	Hopeful	Bored
Happy	Excited	Creative
Nervous	Neutral	Ambitious
Tired	Depressed	Shy
Stressed	Anxious	Embarrassed
Scattered	Angry	Calm

Describe what brought about these feelings

_____

_____

_____

Who did you compliment today and how did that make you feel?

_____

_____

_____

REFLECTIONS

What have you discovered about your life in the last 60 days, and how has it added value to you?

_____

_____

_____

_____

_____

_____

_____

_____

_____

_____

_____

_____

_____

_____

_____

_____

_____

_____

_____

_____

_____

_____

"Gratitude can transform common days into thanksgivings, turn routine jobs into joy, and change ordinary opportunities into blessings."

—William Arthur Ward

Congratulations on completing 60 days of gratefulness. I hope this workbook has added value to your life and brought you a renewed sense of happiness. Keep the positivity going, and no matter what, always be grateful.

There is one final activity you need to complete: The Gratitude Commitment.

The Gratitude Commitment.

Use the chart below to circle one or all of the items per category that you can commit to incorporating into your everyday life. Choose one or as many as you can handle.

Giving Back	Remain Grateful	Self-Care
Compliment Someone Everyday	Continue My Gratitude Jar	Drink Water Daily
Volunteer for a Good Cause	Continue to Journal	Meditate
Donate to Charity	Listen to a Positive Song	Say Affirmations
Buy or Make Someone a Meal	Connect with My Spirituality	Compliment Myself

How has this workbook changed you?

_____

_____

_____

_____

_____

_____

_____

_____

_____

_____

_____

_____

_____

_____

_____

_____

_____

_____

_____

_____

_____

_____

_____

Made in the USA
Middletown, DE
03 February 2023

23913468R00163